# THE
# FINE ART OF
# FLIRTING

*Joyce Jillson*

**Illustrations by Lindsay Harper-duPont**

**F**

A FIRESIDE BOOK
Published by Simon & Schuster
New York London Toronto Sydney Tokyo Singapore

Text Copyright © 1984 by Joyce Jillson
Illustrations Copyright © 1984 by Lindsay Harper-duPont

First Fireside Edition, 1986
Published by Simon & Schuster, Inc.

Rockefeller Center
1230 Avenue of the Americas
New York, New York 10020
FIRESIDE and colophon are registered trademarks
of Simon & Schuster, Inc.
Designed by
Manufactured in the United States of America
Printed by
Bound by

        25  27  29  30  28  26  24
Library of Congress Cataloging in Publication Data
ISBN: 0-671-62752-X

# Contents

## IV   WHEN TO FLIRT

## V   WHERE TO FLIRT

## VI   THE SUCCESSFUL FLIRT

# ♡ I ♡
# *THE BASICS*

# ♡ 1 ♡
## *Flirting 101*

RECENTLY, I RAN INTO A FRIEND OF MINE, A THIRTY-TWO-YEAR-OLD DIVORCÉE WHO IS AVERAGE LOOKING, MODERATELY SUCCESSFUL, AND A MOTHER OF FOUR KIDS. She was just coming home from a weekend business seminar, with three great-looking men pestering her for more of her time. Most of my other friends are pining for ways to find one new man, and here was Cheryl with three.

Did she have a secret?

"I do what every woman thinks she's doing, but which she usually botches up. I flirt."

Come on, I thought. I know Cheryl. She's bright, funny, a good tennis player, but a flirt—never.

But Cheryl told me something other successful flirts later confirmed. "Flirting isn't flirting if it's obvious. If you or any third person can tell, then I'm off target. The men and women who flirt the way they do in the movies are so off base that it leaves the field open for everyday, average people like me who care enough to have perfected the craft.

"Flirting really is a skill like anything else."

Yes, a skill. I learned it and you can too. And once you know the basic moves, your personal refinements will turn this skill into a fine art.

Because I have worked since age sixteen, I missed out on some of the social niceties. The proms, the dating, the parties. But I was lucky. An older friend, Lianne, an outrageous seventy-three-year-old flirt, took me under her wing. She had lived a fascinating life in Europe and was now married, but she still went out of her way to decry the erosion of romance in America.

I met her through her husband, a courtly patrician in his late seventies, who offered to play chess with me. Actually Laurence wasn't *playing* chess with me, he was *teaching* me, although he was always too courteous to call it that. I got progressively better, but never half as good as necessary to beat Laurence.

Then one day, Laurence was out of town, and Lianne and I got a chance to chat. She told me that she and Laurence thought I was improving. Then half in jest, half serious, I said, "He'll never let me get good enough to beat him."

Lianne was startled. "You know you have already surpassed him. He has never spent as much time playing with anyone, man or woman. And you could even beat him, if you would pamper him a little."

That was silly, I thought. Was it really an achievement if I had to use this kind of strategy?

Lianne said, "Life is strategy. You can destroy a building with a bulldozer, or you can be that rare individual who knows how to make a flute resonate so perfectly with the building that the windows crack and the foundations are undermined. You, my dear, are driving a bulldozer; but if you want I will teach you to play the flute."

What Lianne really meant by flute-playing was flirting. She thought people should flirt all the time—with friends, with

youngsters, and especially with the opposite sex. "How do you think I got Laurence?" (Laurence being a Boston Brahmin of some repute), she would brag. And the way she approached teaching me to flirt showed her consummate skill. She never called it "flirting" within my earshot, she called it "European charm."

So one rainy Saturday afternoon when I'd just found out my boyfriend was marching in a peace demonstration with another girl, my basic training in flirting began.

Though I learned, even took notes, about flirting, and thought it was fun, I had no idea how necessary it would become. Then I moved to Los Angeles to work.

Friends told me I would never meet anyone there because people never get out of their cars. Which turned out to be true. For the first couple of months I just worked, and met no one. But the gloom lifted when, in unpacking, I noticed Lianne's notes.

Could they work for me? On a whim, I decided to try them out. (I had nothing to lose, since I didn't know anyone.) But there were several obstacles. I didn't have a car. (I believe this is now against the law for singles in Los Angeles.) And, I don't happen to like the California look in men—muscles, chains, tans, and sushi-breath. This ruled out a lot of eligible men. (In California, eligible is defined as any man whose wife doesn't live with him or whose wife or girl friend lets him have his own private telephone number.)

As a result, I greatly restricted my choice of flirting partners—which you shouldn't do. (I now know that, on the right person, a tan can be very appealing!) Yet . . . I had phenomenal luck. I had so much luck that I would give out my best girl friend's number instead of my own to men, so she could share in the fun. Of course, the fun didn't last long . . . I fell in love. And my women friends took this as evidence of my stinginess, because the phone calls to their numbers ceased.

Lianne has passed away, and her secrets might have been lost if I hadn't been talking with my friend and editor, Barbara Gess, one day. Yes . . . about life and love and romance and . . . flirting.

Barbara asked me to jot down my notes about flirting. But I wanted this book to be a compilation of many different flirting styles, and I wanted this book to be not for women only. So I asked the men and women who are always surrounded by members of the opposite sex for their secrets. Not love secrets or sexual secrets, but *flirting* secrets. I found that between Lianne's old-world charm and the modern-day style of these flirts, there were many similarities. Perhaps, the essence of flirting could, indeed, be set down in writing.

Learning to flirt should be a basic social skill that can be called up when needed. As my friend Cheryl said, "Getting ready for a social event without thinking about how you're going to flirt or if you're going to flirt, is like ironing a dress and then not wearing it. What's the use?"

One legendary fashion plate, a woman who has flirted with every man on both sides of the Atlantic, told me the idea she keeps in the back of her mind. "It's foolish to try to impress, or to make yourself into a sexual image, or to learn the right phrases. None of these work, because what is good for one woman will disgust the next. And goodness knows, every man I've ever known has had a completely different view about what

is sexy. But the enduring trait, the one thing everyone agrees on, is *friendliness*. If you are friendly and warm, no one sees that as anything less than perfection. Why even at my age, women tell me I am flirting with their grandsons, when all I am doing is showing an interest in them. Down deep the core of flirting is friendship. You are putting your best foot forward to encourage a new relationship."

"Then why don't people say that flirting is friendship?" I asked her.

"If we called flirting, friendship, it would be too much good, clean fun, and in romance people want to think they've been a little bit naughty. Besides, with the opposite sex, if things are too understandable and ordinary, everyone loses interest."

A successful male flirt I know says, "Maybe extending friendship is a major part of flirting, but somehow when that friendliness comes from a woman it explodes into something more special than friendship. Or maybe I'm just fantasizing. Either way, it's very pleasant."

If you're wondering why these successful male and female flirts would want to give away their secrets, I'll tell you. Some say it's a boost to their egos to be able to talk about techniques they've applied for years. Others say they aren't worried about finding the field crowded with other flirts. Why? Flirting is so easy and requires so little effort, people won't believe it works.

# ♡ 2 ♡
# The Golden Rule of Flirting

FLIRTING IS A MENTAL GAME. And how you feel about flirting is really the prime asset any successful flirt can have. That's why great flirts observe the Golden Rule of Flirting.

Flirting doesn't require great logic, only diligence. Which is why Descartes wasn't a flirt, but Marilyn Monroe was. If Descartes had been a flirt, instead of writing, "I think, therefore I am," he'd have written, "I flirt, therefore I date."

The Golden Rule of Flirting has evolved from one pivotal fact—that the fine art of flirting is thwarted time and time again by one basic human emotion. Hurt.

Hurt from the past. Imagined hurts in the future. Even hearing, reading about, seeing, and making assumptions about hurt that others have sustained. All these things keep us from moving ahead with our own flirting excursions. Most of us relish these negative associations. We want to hear a blow-by-blow account of Cynthia's breakup or Alan's divorce. The more sensational, the more interested we are. But negative memories inhibit future relationships. At least do yourself the favor of balancing these stories out.

Try incorporating this precept into your flirtatious activities.

> **THE GOLDEN RULE OF FLIRTING**
> **Do unto potential flirting partners as you would have them do unto you—no matter what you think they've already *done* unto you.**

If you don't incorporate the Golden Rule of Flirting into your life, you are like a person with chronic back problems who

'I FLIRT, THEREFORE I DATE'

neglects his exercises. You may be cruising along just fine. Then WHAM. Your lower back or your love life gets thrown out of alignment, and suddenly there's no way you can exercise . . . anything.

Remember new flirting partners will act toward you—eventually—as you act toward them. You can't get out of that pattern.

*An example*: Traci has her eye on the tall, dark man in the three-piece suit standing in the corner, waiting to use the phone. She has initiated eye contact. He hasn't returned her gaze. Traci incorrectly interprets this as lack of interest. Maybe he is concentrating on something else, is nearsighted, has a toothache and is trying to contact an after-hours dentist . . . anything. But Traci takes this as a total, complete rejection. (Right away she is hurting her flirting chances. Good flirts don't get discouraged by one or two rejections. They may let up, but they don't back off.)

Now instead of feeling flirtatious, Traci is angry. This anger keeps other men from approaching her (at least the sensitive ones), for she has activated her internal security system. No one will get through. Her demeanor says that something is wrong. Not a very attractive pose.

Rejecting everyone in close proximity, leaving no one eager to approach her, she is now feeling doubly unwanted. The hurt is building. Wouldn't she love to reject the man in the three-piece suit? You bet. Does she? She would, but she can't. The man is nowhere in sight. But instinctively she pretends that she is snubbing him. She turns her back to that part of the room, putting on the haughty act.

Traci is behaving in this manner because this is the body language she felt this man projected toward her. It is her Traci-like way of imitating him. If the man's actions were as off-putting as hers are, he certainly would not have been a candidate for flirting this evening. Maybe Traci should have sensed that. Instead she decides to get revenge for this supposed rejection by issuing (through her body language) a blanket rejection to every male around. Traci interprets everything from her now distorted point of view.

Poor Traci. She had really wanted to exercise her femininity this evening by flirting. And had succeeded, almost. Bob, seated several tables away, thinks she looks absolutely terrific. Finally Bob gets the courage to stroll by her. He plans to nod, and maybe even say hello.

Bob saunters by and smiles, but Traci is so caught up with rejecting the other man, that she can't see Bob as a fresh, new personality. So Traci turns her shoulders to avoid his grin, and starts talking and laughing with her friend. She'll show him. Bob gets the point, or thinks he does.

Now Bob feels rejected by Traci. Only instead of being a bit more forceful (which would probably snap her out of her negative stance), he slinks back. Bob doesn't act haughty; *his* defeated pose is that of a sad sap. That's the way his old girl friend acted when they had a fight. (And he subconsciously found it pretty effective.) He not only inherited her cat, he also inherited the sad sap act that worked so well on him.

So the fine art of flirting is derailed because of imagined hurt and impersonal rejections. With all these old projections skirting the parameters of male/female encounters, it's a miracle that people connect at all.

But those who do connect with the most ease realize that these dynamics are at play. Leave past romantic partners and current hurts out of your flirting plan. Stop trying to get back at them. By basing your flirting attitude solely on how successful *you* are in treating *others*, your aura of attractiveness and invisible magnetism will expand.

Like money in a bank, flirting pays interest (although there are penalties for premature withdrawals). So I suggest that you sign up your own, personal I.F.A. account. An Investment Flirting Account. The great part is that you can draw on it far before retirement, it's not taxed ever, and there is no minimum deposit.

Follow the Golden Rule of Flirting and you'll have a storehouse of memories and a treasure trove of good experiences. And you'll receive more Valentine cards than anyone in your neighborhood.

# ♡ 3 ♡

# *The 3 Flirting Basics*

## (What the Boy and Girl Scouts Didn't Tell You)

NO MATTER WHAT YOU THINK, TO BE A GREAT FLIRT IT'S NOT NECESSARY TO BE DEVASTATINGLY ATTRACTIVE, RICH, SMOOTH, OR GOOD AT BATTING YOUR EYELASHES. These assets are just window dressing for the successful flirt and pale in comparison to the three flirting basics.

To master the fine art of flirting you must decide you *want* to be a good flirt. You must acknowledge to yourself that this is important. (Let's see. I need new brakes, must finish the boss's report, and would like to flirt. Priorities: Well, if I don't get new brakes, I could crash and never get a chance to finish that report. Flirting? I'll do it next weekend.)

Wrong choice. You've already done that for too many weekends in a row.

Think of flirting as exercise. Like exercising, it is always tough to do at the beginning. You are out-of-shape and the prospect of exercising may not have the appeal it does for those fitness fanatics who look so good in their sporting outfits. Therefore, at the outset, you must decide that looking and feeling good is worth the enormous initial efforts.

To learn the three flirting basics, register yourself at *The Fine Art of Flirting* exercise salon—**The Flirtout\***.

In the beginning all exercise is tough. **The Flirtout** exercise routine is no exception. But just as you develop physical muscle through repetition, so will you develop social muscle: the emotional and social resiliency that makes a flirt not just good—but great.

---

\*The Flirtout got its name because you can't flirt at home. You must go out.

You'll need exercise clothes (your flirting outfit), lessons (this book), and good nutrition (especially Vitamin "E" for you over-achievers). During the first days your muscles (heart?) may ache, so don't overdo. And remember to breathe out and in. Holding your breath, whether waiting for someone to come to you or as part of your aerobics, is wrong. At **The Flirtout,** we promote self-reliance.

> **THE THREE FLIRTING BASICS:**
> 1. **Be Smart.**
> 2. **Be Patient.**
> 3. **Be Prepared.**

## ♡ 1. Be Smart

Flirts must act intelligently. In flirtatious circumstances, it's not enough to have all the lines and the mannerisms of flirting down pat. You must also be smart enough to assess a situation, so you know when flirting is appropriate. By using your logical mind along with your sensual feelings, you not only save yourself a lot of trouble and time, but you keep your options open longer.

Being smart regarding flirting, isn't being sharp-tongued, critical, or pseudo-intellectual. You must simply be alert. How? By constantly assessing the plus and minus of a potential flirtation. And the time to be analytical is *before* you flirt, not *during* a flirtatious encounter.

One of the benefits of superior flirting is that you are able to pick and choose with a discerning eye, and your past experiences can tip you off to minor problems that you want to avoid. Pity the poor man or woman who only flirts occasionally, for though they need the most protection from unsavory flirting partners, they are the least likely to see the warning signals.

Being smart means knowing ahead of time what you want to

accomplish. Look before you leap. Observe others. Listen. Be smart enough to know that one rejection or triumph isn't the end-all of your social life. Exchange information with others. Don't expect a miracle, and act only in accordance with your moral principles. Smart flirts not only don't hate themselves in the morning, they don't hate themselves even that same night, for they rarely regret an action they took.

Being smart about flirting is not the same as projecting an "elitist" attitude. That is flirting suicide. (And there are too many flirting casualties already. Warren Beatty has seen to that.) But smart means that you know yourself well enough to tell if some woman is handing you a line. Or if a man tells you that the woman in the slinky blue dress that he has to take home is his sister, you, as a smart flirt, won't be shocked when they passionately kiss while getting into a cab. (However, if the girl appears very young, call the authorities and save him and her a lifetime of psychiatric treatment.)

A smart flirt doesn't give his or her flirting partners too many chances to go wrong. As one woman said, "If I permit a new flirting partner to make a fool out of himself, what has either of us gained? I treat a man the way I treated my daughter's first pair of shoes. I gilded them. The shoes can never be used again . . . but the man . . . maybe."

But most important, smart flirts are socially comfortable and accomplished enough that they needn't rely on alcohol or chemicals to make them sparkle. They keep control over their own actions, which is what makes them so successful with the opposite sex.

## ♡ 2. Be Patient

It's hard to wait, especially for love. However, like any other exercise salon, **The Flirtout** holds classes only at certain times. And not the times you dictate.

So flirts who succeed are the most patient people in the world. They don't push potential flirting partners when they're not in the mood. They don't spring their most humorous and endearing anecdote on someone who has just suffered a personal loss—whether they are mourning a lost love, job, or car key.

As a patient flirt, you are sure enough of your flirtatious skills to know that waiting only improves your chances. To the person you are flirting with there is nothing so appealing as someone who thinks he is worth waiting for. (Probably his mother

was the last person who felt that way.) If you appear unhurried and give the impression you are not going to be dissuaded from your objective of impressing him, he will very likely give in to your initial invitations—because being with you seems inevitable. And who can resist a flirting companion who says in so many ways that you are worth her patient efforts?

Patient doesn't mean lazy. At **The Flirtout** instructors say that increasing your social profile is essential for you to have success. Patient flirting means maintaining a repeated presence in the life of your flirting partner. This can be done by phone, by sending a birthday card, or by just being around their favorite hangout. (**The Flirtout** teaches these skills.) Patient flirting isn't obsessive. If you are patient, you know it isn't necessary to call every day or even once a week. You create your own flirtatious profile, by just being around. (**The Flirtout** guarantees that this passive flirting approach is one of the most effective for establishing romantic contact with someone you think of as "marriage material."

## ♡ 3. Be Prepared

Do you really want to wring every flirting opportunity from life? Then, think of yourself as being on red-alert for flirting. Here's a tip from one very sought-after woman, a lawyer in Chicago. Before graduating from law school, Lori was an actress. She actually put herself through law school by modeling.

What does this have to do with flirting? This very successful flirt told me she learned a valuable romantic lesson from her actress/model days.

"When I was modeling, I could get a call from my agent at any time—day, night, weekends. And since my appearance was what I was selling, it had to be perfect. So when I was out shopping, going to a movie, walking my dog, I always looked as good as I could, because I might have to go to an interview from wherever I was. This forced me to upgrade my whole style of life. And it's helped me meet men, because I got in the habit of looking and feeling my best. Now, I never have to avoid a new encounter because I'm not at my best. If other women realized what they were missing when they go grocery shopping, they'd spend the time looking good then, instead of just focusing on date nights."

That's right. Flirting takes place most successfully when you least expect it. Flirting is to love what *Candid Camera* was to television. So make being prepared a daily habit. Always be ready to say, "hi," to accept a compliment, to speak to someone new.

Preparation takes two forms:

*Being physically prepared.* Which doesn't mean you have to wear tons of makeup or wear your newest designer jeans. You may be far more interesting without these disguises. But you should be presentable. If you see a neighbor or business colleague, you shouldn't want to shrink away. **The Flirtout** rule for clothes is very inexpensive—one good steam iron can cover a lot of dressing sins. Some flirts carry one in the trunk of their cars, along with other flirting accessories like tennis rackets, dancing shoes, and Listerine.

*Being emotionally prepared.* If you are serious about flirting, you mustn't carry your troubles with you all the time. Needlessly mulling over problems turns you inward, and to flirt you need an outward focus.

**The Flirtout** recommends this little tidbit. Remember the phrase "Wrap up your troubles in an old kitbag, and smile, smile, smile"? Well, at **The Flirtout** we have a basket, and before class every man and woman is asked to drop in the name of someone of the opposite sex who has disappointed them. This has released a lot of hostility, and one man actually raided the basket looking for new dating partners.

Being prepared also means having alternatives. If you are flirting and you have just struck out, do you have other plans made so you don't dwell on this disappointment? Flirting always presents new surprises and dilemmas, but the more you do of it, the more confidence you'll have.

Lastly, preparation means knowing what you want from a flirtatious encounter. In fact, being specific about the outcome you'd like may be the *best* preparation of all.

## ♡ 4 ♡
# Getting Results

### KNOW WHAT YOU WANT

The fastest way to get results in flirting is to determine your own flirting goals. So ask yourself. Do you want to have your sexuality reaffirmed, marry, get a date for a prom, discover new interests, get someone to pick up a check, attract a new partner who likes the same vacations you do, find someone to car-pool with, start your own private twosome of "parents without partners," eat home-cooked meals, find a reason to clean the sheets, or what? The list is endless. But *your* list shouldn't be.

Here are the goals of some well-practiced flirts:

"I want to get encouragement for my diet. If I just stayed around my boyfriend, I don't think I'd be as motivated."

"Flirting provides me with a new sport. And since I have tennis elbow, I rate my flirting prowess the way I used to rate my serve. So far I'm not smashing the ball to center court, but at least I'm no longer lobbing."

"I flirt because I hate to pay for cabs."

"Why do I flirt? Because if I didn't, I'd have to settle for the guys I work with, who are real jerks."

"Flirting is my college education, and I like the fact you don't have to select your major until the very last day."

"I flirt because there's more to life than news, weather, and sports."

"Flirting. I guess I do it because it makes me feel good to be able to take the initiative."

A nurse says, "Sure I flirt. It's the only way those male doctors can be civilized."

"Reasons for flirting? Naturally I'm looking for someone to marry, but I always flirt when I need advice, because you're sure to get it."

"My flirting is really an outgrowth of being friendly. And since I want to be faithful to my husband, this is my way of helping him get new insurance accounts. That's what I tell him anyway."

"I flirt because I'm a policeman. If I didn't, no one would like me."

"Flirting for me is one of the best physical outlets. It's great in winter when I can't swim because the pool isn't heated."

"When I flirt, I realize that what I say is important; it's a great morale booster for a housewife."

"The reason I flirt is for my wife. I tell her it keeps my motor running until I get home."

"Honestly, I flirt because I'm lonely, and flirting puts me in contact with others."

"I flirt because my girl friend always tells me what I do wrong. When I flirt, I realize how many women appreciate a little male imperfection!"

Most people cite meeting people, new relationships, new experiences, more ease with the opposite sex, and those dreaded single supplements as reasons for flirting. (Note to restaurateurs: Many singles said they flirted just so they wouldn't have to eat alone.)

If these are some of your goals, too, make your reasons more specific. Write them down—although you should probably hide them in case you strike pay dirt; your pleasure will be spoiled if your love finds this list.

## KNOW WHAT KIND OF FLIRTING PARTNER YOU WANT

Getting results demands that you select a flirting partner who fills your needs. It's a waste of time to be fabulously flirtatious with a woman who reeks of cheap perfume if your flirting objective is to meet a woman who will help you entertain rich industrialists for business. Should you be in the nightclub business, however, she could be a plus.

So to get results, you have to do 50 percent of the work ahead of time.

## Plan a Flirting Menu

You can't order every dish at every meal, so each time, savor a different treat. Make your flirting menu diverse, but don't overburden the kitchen. Stick with one basic cuisine, as too much diversity might overwhelm those who can fulfill your flirtatious orders.

How do you do this? You continually talk about what type of man or woman you are looking for. Not in a way that denotes desperation—just to let others know what your preferences are. If this seems too embarrassing, pretend you are talking about someone else.

As a test, admit one day that your ideal man is short, single, and flies an airplane. (If you make him married, you'll have every pilot camping on your doorstep . . . plus a few flight controllers who are still looking for a woman to help with the expense of retraining for a new career.) You'll be inundated with people who have friends who have friends who fit this requirement. Try this and you'll find that it does pay to advertise.

You'll find that you are suddenly surrounded by more people who meet your criteria than you thought possible. (This could be because YOU see more of these positive traits, since you have clearly decided what you want to focus on. Or it could be that your announcement has made it easy for friends to be matchmakers.)

Additionally, new people who know what you are seeking are more likely to highlight those elements of their own personality which mesh with your requirements. Tell friends you want to date an athlete, and you can bet every man who shows up at your door will be wearing Adidas and a sweatband, probably both. Let a woman know through the grapevine that you are looking for an "ultra-feminine creature," and your date will undoubtedly wear ruffles *somewhere* on her body.

## KNOW WHAT YOUR FLIRTING PARTNER WANTS

Let's dispense with the platitudes:

Men flirt so they can bed as many women as possible.
Women flirt so they can find someone to marry them.

Okay. So maybe we can't dispense with them completely, since both phrases have grains of *partial* truth in them. But people mistakenly give these reasons more weight than is necessary. Don't you do this.

To get almost immediate results from flirting, you must be aware of the supplemental needs your flirting partner wants satisfied. Most people want increased self-esteem, a feeling of being sought after, and relief from social isolation. But you expert flirts will want to throw in one plus. I always suggest that you give a man or woman you are flirting with something they can relate to their office cronies the next day. Information, statistics—better yet, anecdotes, experiences, a joke. These co-workers then become *your* flirting allies. At the very least, one of them does, as every work place has an office gossip. This person will bring your name up time and time again, giving you a continued flirting presence.

If you incorporate the satisfaction of these needs into **your** flirting game plan, you'll get results because you are, in fact, giving others the results **they** want from a flirtation. And in turn, the next concession will be made in your direction. (One of the bonuses of flirting.) As one flirtatious man said, "I make her feel good, then I let her reciprocate by fixing me dinner."

# ♡ 5 ♡
# *Are You in the Right Mood to Flirt?*

·IN THE MOOD·

1.  Do you have a twinkle in your eye? Would someone describe you as sparkling?
2.  Can you momentarily put personal problems aside while you flirt?
3.  Can you refrain from asking a member of the opposite sex to comment on a recent romantic argument?
4.  *For Women:* If a man seems uninterested in your feminine wiles, would you still consider having him as a friend?
    *For Men:* Would you consider introducing a woman who turned you down, to your best buddy who thinks she's adorable?
5.  After visiting your neighborhood bookstore, if you return *without* the book you need but *with* several phone numbers of promising flirting partners, do you consider the trip a success?
6.  Are you flirting for your personal pleasure, rather than to get back at someone?

7. If someone comes over for a drink, do you have something besides a protein-powder milk shake to serve them?

8. If you have pictures of an "ex" at your home, do you know their exact locations, so you can scoop them all up when the doorbell rings, before you answer it?

9. Do you feel good about your body? If not, can you at least forgo discussing your diet/exercise/health problems for an evening?

10. When a new companion visits you, will you be satisfied if that person plays with your cat/dog/gerbil for only ten minutes?

11. If you have children, do you wait till your companion leaves before hearing the kids' evaluation of your new friend's marriage potential?

12. Do you remember faces more easily than names, and never forget what someone you dated looks like? (Forgetting the name is part of a single person's survival strategy.)

13. Can you graciously accept a compliment?

14. *Women:* If you looked like Victoria Principal, would you still flirt?
    *Men:* If you looked like Tom Selleck, would you still flirt?

15. If someone rejects you, are you grown-up enough to whisper your insulting retort, rather than yell it?

16. If you buy someone a drink or coffee or a snack, and the other person suddenly gets up and leaves; would you stay and finish the refreshment by yourself?

17. Are you indifferent to social status when you flirt? In other words, are you absolutely sure that you would be just as bold flirting with a peer as you are with people you imagine to be beneath you in class, education, financial stature, or appearance?

18. If, when flirting, someone asks for your telephone number and you don't want to give it, do you think it's important to help that person save face?

19. Naturally *you* don't make this social gaffe. But . . . at some chance encounter or social gathering, if someone should refer to you as "Hon," "Dear," "Bud," "Sweetheart," or a nickname you detest, can you discreetly let this pass without making a federal case out of what could be an innocent slip?

**20.** Are you comfortable responding to the flirtatious actions of a member of the opposite sex, even when you feel you're not looking your best?

**Scoring:** If you answered yes to 17–20 questions, you are absolutely confident about yourself, your sexuality, and your attractiveness. You probably are married.

If you answered yes to 13–16 questions, you are a magnetic, charismatic person. The marriage partners of those people who have 17–20 "yes" answers find you very alluring.

If you answered yes to 9–12 questions, you have been to too many communication workshops and tell-it-like-it-is personal-growth seminars.

With 5–8 "yes" answers you are smart enough to know that flirting can help you, but too scared to try. You probably will hide this book, so no one will see it.

With from 0–4 "yes" answers, you bought this book thinking it was about fishing, not flirting.

# ♡ II ♡
# WHO FLIRTS?

# ♡ 6 ♡
# *Great Flirts in History*

THE DUCHESS OF ALBA

Adam and Eve
Samson and Delilah
Madame Bovary
Isadora Duncan
Florence Nightingale
Tutankhamen
Eva Perón
Robin Hood and Maid Marian
Cleopatra and Mark Antony
  (but not Caesar, he was a dud)
Wild Bill Hickok
Hester Prynne
Peter Pan
Duchess of Alba
  (posed nude for Goya)
Mona Lisa
Picasso

Circe
Snow White and two
  of the Dwarfs
Sarah Bernhardt
Catherine the Great
Alexander the Great
Casanova
Henry VIII
Thomas Jefferson
Venus de Milo
Marilyn Monroe
Rosie the Riveter
Betsy Ross
Lothario
Sigmund Freud
Josephine Bonaparte
William Randolph Hearst

# ♡ 7 ♡
# A Who's Who of Great Flirts
## (But Without the Embarrassing Background Information)

James Bond

Jacqueline Onassis

Henry Kissinger

Daisy Mae

Louis Jourdan, Alain Delon, Jean-Louis Trintignant (and all French men except Mitterand)

Any Miss Congeniality

Mrs. Paul, Sara Lee, (Mrs.) Swanson, Dolly Madison (and anyone who puts her name on food specialties)

Joan Collins

Brooke, Panty, and the other Shields girls

All the Hemingways

William F. Buckley

Duchess of Windsor

Coco Chanel

Alice in Wonderland (her naiveté was very appealing)

Margaret Thatcher

Any ex-wife of Johnny Carson

The Motels

Dr. Pepper

Anyone who writes a fitness book and poses for the pictures personally

Frank Sinatra

Mary Cunningham

Any man married to a movie star who suddenly gets to direct a film

J.R. Ewing

Radio psychologists

Halston

Superman, Batman, Zorro, and any man who wears a cape, especially Dracula

# ♡ 8 ♡
# *A Day in the Life of a Flirt*

NATURAL FLIRTS WAKE UP WITH JUST ABOUT ANYTHING ON THEIR MINDS EXCEPT FLIRTING. I said "natural" flirts. But like blonds, the so-called "natural" flirt has had her native endowments enhanced with a little help from the experts. If you can spot a flirt, or a dye-job, it's the work of an amateur. So for those of you who don't have an expert flirtatious friend to model yourselves after, here's a day in the life of one of my favorite, outrageous female flirts.

## A DAY WITH MARGIE

**6:45 A.M.** Wake-up call. She doesn't receive it; she makes it. To Bill, her ex-husband. Margie knows that an ex can serve as a last-minute escort. Besides, it's good to have someone to confide in about their dog's antics.

**6:48 A.M.** Wake-up call. From Jerry. Jerry lives in another city, and it's a nice way to keep in touch. She tells Jerry she misses him, and then gets up.

**6:53 A.M.** She dresses and runs to exercise class.

**7:05 A.M.** At exercise class, she asks one of the men in class for help. Is her tummy-tuck position right? Margie knows it is—she once taught this class. Still, people like to give advice, and this interaction is sure to elicit a response after class.

**7:49 A.M.** Man in exercise class asks her for coffee. She declines because of work. He offers a rain check. Margie knows that rain checks never materialize unless you "seed your own clouds." Margie explains that she doesn't go to exercise class here that often. They exchange phone numbers.

*Note:* Margie rotates her exercising schedule, rarely showing up at the same place more than once every two weeks.

Says she, "The variety is good for my soul." Not to mention her flirting!

**8:05 A.M.** She rushes home to eat and dress for a breakfast meeting with a client. Margie has strawberry yogurt. She knows the purpose of a breakfast meeting is not to consume one-third of your total daily calories. At breakfast meetings, Margie has other objectives in mind.

**8:45 A.M.** Breakfast. Margie walks into her favorite hotel dining room. She knows the maître d'. Good flirts like to operate in familiar territory. Plus, a maître d's assistance can be invaluable. Once this particular maître d' introduced her to an Arab sheik. Today he points out a new man to her who just moved into the hotel. "I think he's going through a divorce," the maître d' speculates. Margie makes a mental note to come back some morning—alone.

**9:30 A.M.** The meeting goes very well, and she gets the account. Her breakfast companion is not, however, a flirting prospect — this is business, and, besides, he is married. Nevertheless, Margie is charming and cordial, so he leaves expecting to see her again for another meeting. "Let's do that after we get started working on your account." Margie may mix business and pleasure, but not before she's *sure* of her business.

**10:15 A.M.** Before work she rushes to pick up a newspaper. At the newsstand, a very appealing man takes a second glance at her. As she chats with the newsstand operator, she makes sure to mention where she works, loud enough for the stranger to hear. Margie guesses there's a fifty-fifty chance he'll call.

**10:25 A.M.** Upstairs, Margie makes sure her dress-for-success uniform isn't too severe. She unbuttons the vest for a more approachable look. Her first meeting is with the other department managers. Margie likes one of them and compliments his suggestions in the meeting (sincerely, of course). She takes notes so they can talk later.

**10:45 A.M.** She phones a male friend who works at a competing firm. Margie likes to stay in touch with her professional peers. Especially since this man is peerless. They set up a lunch date for the next day.

**11:00 A.M.** A temporary business consultant sits in on the meeting to look over a new advertising layout. Margie asks how long he'll be working there. When he says only another week-and-a-half, Margie gives him a big smile. She asks, "Would you mind calling me after the study is completed? I'd love to know some of the findings, so I can put them to use immediately." Then she confides, "I'm in line for a promotion, but it's close. My doing this on my own could really help my chances."

The man gives her his card. But since Margie doesn't want to take his time from business, she suggests he take her home telephone number. "Just in case you have any questions while you're writing up your report this weekend."

**12:30 P.M.** Lunch. With some women friends. Margie knows that Suzanne wants to fix her up with a pal of her fiancé. Margie steers the conversation in that direction by suggesting that she and Suzanne get together for dinner sometime.

**12:40 P.M.** A telephone is brought to their table. This makes a huge impression on a man Margie's had her eye on for months. He's a bit older and always lunches in this restaurant. Since he's only a table away, Margie asks the waiter what "that man" is having—it looks so good. (She knows because she changed her seat to be directly in his line of vision.) This brings the waiter to his side, and the man and Margie exchange a brief glance. Margie smiles, and says "Thanks." She orders the halibut, which she hates, but this serves a dual purpose—she also doesn't want to eat much at lunch. Ordering something she hates keeps her from overindulging. A little trick Margie shared with me.

**1:25 P.M.** Lunch is over. Margie goes to get her coat from the checkroom, waiting until another very attractive man is just ahead of her. While the checkroom woman gets his overcoat, Margie asks him if he feels safe checking his briefcase there. She says she's always afraid to do that, because if she lost her files on the Dumont account, she'd be in big trouble.

Triumph, thinks Margie. He asks about the Dumont account, but Margie can say no more. "Corporate secrets at Company XYZ," she says, skillfully getting in the name of her firm. They wait for a cab together. He lets her take the first one—and with a warm smile, she promises, "See you soon."

**2:00 P.M.** She returns a few personal calls. And makes one to a man who just received a promotion. Before making that call, though, Margie checks with the New York Stock Exchange to find out what his favorite stock is selling at. She wants to have something to say beyond "Congratulations."

**2:12 P.M.** Roger calls for a date Friday evening. She tells him she'd love to, but she'll be out of town. Margie *is* going away for the weekend, but she wants Roger to call again. She prolongs the conversation just a bit, to let Roger know she remembers that he was in the midst of purchasing a video recorder. Playing back personal details is one way to let a man know he hasn't struck out and should call again.

**2:30 P.M.** A disgruntled client calls. This is where Margie must use all her charm and talent, perfected through flirting. She tells the woman that she wants to help. At the end of the call, the client has decided to give the company another month to get the problem solved.

**4:35 P.M.** A colleague from another department asks her for a drink. Margie agrees, but puts a time limit on the meeting. "I'd love to. Let's do it at 5:15 because I have to leave for an appointment by 6:00."

**5:00 P.M.** Margie fixes her makeup and finishes her work. She says hello to the man still sitting in the reception area. "Can I help you?" Margie inquires. "You're the first person who has asked," he replies. Margie makes a note to take care of the problem tomorrow. She gets the man the packet of data he requested, and smiles. "Call me personally if there's another problem. I'll put you through to the right person." Margie always remembers the one-in-thirty rule. "I don't necessarily expect anything, but I sure keep all my options open."

**5:15 P.M.** The drinks date. Margie likes the business colleague, but he's not her type. They talk about various subjects, and she asks him to introduce her to a man he waved to at the bar. A few comments later, Margie realizes this man is not for her either. But she offers her card. As Margie later clarified, "That man may have a friend. Besides, he works for a company I might want to work for some day."

**6:00 P.M.** Margie leaves to buy her brother a tie for his birthday. She goes to the most expensive men's store in town. "Of course, I wouldn't buy it here; things are so overpriced. But I get to learn about value, and some of the men are just fabulous about helping me with my selections." She does get help from a distinguished older man who seems very nice. Suddenly his wife pops up. Margie has crossed this bridge before. She asks the wife for her opinion. "Once I did this, and they were both so sweet. They invited me to their home for dinner where I met the most fabulous man from the United Nations."

**6:30 P.M.** Card shop. Margie gets a birthday card for her brother and sees a funny card that is perfect to send to a man. She buys one birthday card, and seventeen humor cards. Why seventeen? That's all they had.

**7:00 P.M.** She turns on the nightly news and her hot rollers. Margie is ready to do some dancing. She and her best friend are double-dating. Tonight Margie can't flirt. Her rule is — when out on a date, it is gauche to flirt. There are exceptions, however—when she and the man go Dutch, Margie flirts half the time.

**10:00 P.M.** Home. Then out again. Margie ventures out to her favorite all-night newspaper stand. She picks up the *Wall Street Journal* just as an interesting-looking man is buying his. They talk, and he tells her where he lives. (A sign of a single man, Margie says.) He walks her home. Unfortunately Margie is stuck buying the *Wall Street Journal* when she really wanted the *Ladies' Home Journal.*

**11:00 P.M.** Call friends. She finds out how David's job interview went, checks on Lance's new car, and makes sure that Robin is taking his vitamins. Of course, Margie has call-waiting service on her phone. Because when it comes to telephone calls, Margie knows it is better to receive than to give.

**11:30 P.M.** Bed. She puts her telephone answering machine on. Flirt, or no flirt, there are some people she'd pick up the phone for. Even at 3 A.M. Her mother, Larry, and Don.

**3:00 A.M.** The phone rings. She has the volume up and hears that it is Don. Margie picks up. "Don. No, you're not disturbing me. We're fine." There is silence at the other end. Margie answers his silent question. "It's just me and the dog. Silly." Flirts always enjoy playing games. "Saturday night? I was going away for the weekend." Apparently Don is apologizing. "Maybe I can make it." Margie mentally decides to spend the weekend with Don. After all, good flirts are flexible.

# ♡ 9 ♡
# *The Married Flirt*
## (Or How to Keep the Home Fires Burning)

YOU DON'T HAVE TO BE SINGLE TO BE A FLIRT. Some of the happiest married couples find that flirting keeps the excitement going in a relationship. Flirting provides a harmless escape hatch. It is non-sexist, non-discriminating, and non-fattening. (As for dieting, flirts get so much feedback on how they look that married flirts find staying in shape easier. "Maybe my husband doesn't care or see my tummy bulge, but my flirting partners will.")

As one formerly married flirt told me, "I flirted with my hus-

JUST-MARRIED FLIRTS

band before we married, I flirted after we split. I think I would still be married if I had flirted during our marriage."

Men say that having a wife who flirts isn't at all disconcerting. "I get the benefit of all the romance and sexual energies, so if some other man's going to make my wife happy; that's good for me."

Flirting is not revenge. You don't flirt to make your spouse feel insecure. That's not flirting, that's taunting. But you do have fun. You enjoy being around others of the opposite sex, and your pleasure rubs off on your partner.

Married flirts are usually able to keep the passion alive in their marriages longer than others are. But their flirting is not done secretly. It is all out in the open. Married flirters who are "discreet" are called "cheaters."

Here are two types of married male flirts: One said that when he really liked his wife, he flirted *in front* of her, so that she knew he wanted to go home with her only. The other said, "I knew I had lost interest in my wife when I started flirting in the office and behind her back."

# ♡ 10 ♡
# *Flirtophobia*
## (The Fear of Flirting)

WHEN THE TOPIC OF FLIRTING COMES UP, PEOPLE DIVIDE THEM-SELVES INTO TWO CATEGORIES:

1. Those who say they flirt.
2. Those who say they CAN'T.

What if you're in the second group? What if you're afraid to flirt? (Anyone *can* flirt; so admit it, you're not certain you *want* to.) What if you'd like to flirt but you've tried before (once) and things didn't work out?

Then you've received a lot of misinformation about flirting. Or maybe not enough correct information. Or maybe you heard negative comments from someone who was jealous of you.

To flirt, all you have to do is take action. Almost any action at all—with the right mental attitude—is a flirtatious gesture. As William James said, "The emotions are not always subject to reason . . . but they are always subject to action." So all you need do is act—flirtatiously—any way, any time, any place, any method. The results will be there.

· DO NOT BE SCARED TO FLIRT ·

If you're afraid, then call it something else. Call it being friendly. That's what flirting really is anyway. Go out and be especially friendly to the people you see. Get your feet wet by saying you just want to meet *people*—not members of the opposite sex.

After all, no one is judging you. Flirting is a solitary activity. Only *you* will know if you fail. But before you chalk any potential flirtation up to failure or success, consider this interesting story.

A successful woman flirt I know is very selective about the men she will flirt with. Only the best are halfway good enough for her. Well, there was a man we all thought would never have a chance with her. He was rather crass, not as intelligent or well dressed as she, and yet he was head over heels in love with this woman. He flirted with her until his eyes almost popped out of his head. Nothing. He called; her secretary wouldn't put him through. He sent flowers on Valentine's Day. We all thought he was an absolute flirting failure.

However, one day he was seen having lunch with her. The next day he was seen walking her to her car, and soon they were an "item." We finally asked her what won her over. Was it his personality? What?

"His honesty. He didn't make any bones about what he was doing. I didn't have to try and figure him out; after all that time I knew him. Which was funny, because then I felt I knew him more than he knew me. And that made me try harder to please him."

If that man had been afraid to keep flirting and had interpreted all the signals as rejection, he would have thought he had failed. But he won. And won big because he looked at the broader picture, not the tiny little incidents.

Here's another mental trick that may help potential flirts. Pretend you are practicing anthropology amongst the natives. You are trying to fathom how and why certain humans interact playfully with one another. (What are these ritualistically clothed individuals doing? And why are they smiling so much?) Of course, as a true scientist of human nature, you'll not only want to observe, you'll want to participate. Not because you are a flirt (oh, not at all), but because you're just trying to decipher the strange language that some sexual creatures speak.

Flirting, like slang, is catchy. Subconsciously, your body picks up the language, and before you realize it you'll have passed your initiation rites into the group.

Finally, if you're still scared to flirt, don't despair. Everyone is at various times. The flirts who appear confident have just learned to hide this discomfort better than most.

# ♡ 11 ♡
# *Are You Really Ready to Flirt?*

BECAUSE FLIRTING IS AS MUCH AN ATTITUDE AS IT IS A SET OF ACTIONS, HOW YOU THINK ABOUT IT IS AS IMPORTANT AS HOW YOU DO IT. You need delicacy, patience, and confidence. Keep reminding yourself that by flirting, *you* are doing someone a favor, since you are opening the lines of communications. And if you really need a boost, remember that everyone fails occasionally. The Duchess of Windsor, an accomplished flirt known as "Mrs. Simpson," failed. Her obvious, undisciplined, flirtatious antics with the king of England cost him his throne; a really successful, subtle flirt could have convinced Parliament that she should be queen.

Find out if you're ready to flirt.

| READY TO FLIRT | NOT READY TO FLIRT |
|---|---|
| You regularly scent your room with potpourri. | When guests are expected, you enlist the aid of a two-year-old Airwick. |
| On vacations, you hope to meet a new love. | You'd like to meet a new love before your trip, so you can save the cost of the single supplement. |
| At the supermarket, you are friendly and talkative. | At the supermarket, you blame the checker for the high prices. |
| You just got a promotion or raise and want to celebrate. | You lost your job and want to drown your troubles. |

| READY TO FLIRT | NOT READY TO FLIRT |
|---|---|
| An old love has ended and you know you'll survive. | An old love has ended, and you'd like another opinion about what went wrong with the affair. |
| At self-help seminars, you have the most fun at the breaks talking to people. | At self-help seminars, you remark that the group is a bunch of losers, and often request a refund. |
| You freely talk to neighbors and share household items. | On garbage day, you accuse the neighbors of going through your private trash. |
| You let other people read your magazines when you finish. | You let others read your magazines, waiting until they are six months old before ripping off your address labels and giving them away. |
| You are not emotionally starved. | You are emotionally starved, but hide it by being self-contained, or by discussing the decay in social values. |
| You carry coins in case you want to call and notify someone you'll be a few minutes late. | You always carry pennies, in case you have to split a dinner check. |

# ♡ 12 ♡
## *Your Flirting Profile*

EVERYONE HAS THE ABILITY TO FLIRT. As little children, we do it naturally. Unfortunately, all that charm, grace, and whimsy usually gets lost somewhere along the path to adulthood. Somehow, we forget that flirting is as simple as getting along with others, enthralling them with our sensuality and attractiveness, our humor and common sense.

To sharpen your flirting profile, all you have to do is unearth the treasures in your own personality, by rediscovering all those alluring traits you've been suppressing. The more you develop, improve, and understand your own flirtatious assets, the sooner you can reap the benefits of flirting. Here are some tips to get you started.

### BE POPULAR

Your mother was right. It can't hurt to learn to play the piano. Because there are times in life when a skill, talent, or personality trait will give you an edge over others. While Mom was wrong that the piano was the panacea for all your social ills, she was right in trying to give you an edge.

I'll bet she never dreamed it would help you flirt. Popularity is to flirting what protein is to food. It is the element of regeneration, rejuvenation . . . really, it is the brain-food of flirting. Because through your own well-cultivated popularity, you can ease your way into flirting situations that Mata Hari would shy away from.

But if your fairy godmother didn't make you president of your homeroom in the fourth grade, or homecoming queen, or captain of the football team, you don't have to be relegated to the sidelines forever. Popularity can be learned. Here's how to improve your overall popularity with both men and women, a definite asset for anyone who flirts:

**1. Be the bearer of good news.** People love to hear about other people, and the information needn't be earth shattering. If a friend got a promotion, call and let another pal know. Does your charter plane have room for one more person on a trip to the Caribbean? Let others know. And one of the best ways is to call friends or even acquaintances with news of a job-opening that you've heard about.

**2. Be a good listener.** You needn't offer advice (it's actually best if you don't), but learn to sit through a pal's blow-by-blow replay of a recent argument at work. This rule becomes extremely potent when you allow someone of the opposite sex to unburden their romantic problems on your shoulders. Instant intimacy develops, and if you can bide your time during this "recovery" phase, you are definitely in a strong position to turn this platonic relationship into a passionate one.

If you have no idea how to be a good listener, just hold back every other responsive remark you're thinking of. Not every one. Learn how to nod, say "uh hum," and generally let the person know you are keeping pace with his thoughts. Beware of interrupting. Let someone finish his thought, especially if it seems like a personal one. Most people will go on and on, which is why talk radio stations find that commercials actually make callers *more* interesting, because their air time is limited.

And if all else fails, get earplugs—that way you'll hear snippets of the conversation, enough to respond, but not enough to get bored.

**3. Go out of your way to meet new people.** Don't worry if they like you. Don't worry if you like them. All you need to do is mingle. Not talk. Not know anyone. Not be the best looking. Frankly, you don't even have to know the language. Haven't you seen spy movies where two people used this technique?

Why do it? Just the act of seeing and being around different groups of people gives others the impression you are popular.

**4. Pick up the telephone.** When in doubt, dial. People love to hear the phone ring; that's why they have those ubiquitous answering machines, so they won't miss one solitary message. Why else do people have so many telephone extensions, telephone pagers, and car phones?

Flirts play on this foible. First find out how many extensions or phone lines a potential flirting partner has. You do this by saying you hear static on the line. (Since the phone company split up, everyone has this.) Then ask. Based on the answer, you can tell how anxious someone is to hear from you, and how much you can use your telephone privileges.

*Just one phone:* This person spends all his time at his club, office, or parents' house. Not a good candidate for phone flirting.

*Two or more phone lines:* Call day, night, holidays, mornings. They want—no, strike that—they NEED to talk. Communication is essential. You know you have struck a flirtatious bell when your flirting partner gives you the *other* number (usually that number is reserved for outgoing calls.) Bingo!

*No phone?* This person is married and not telling you. But show that you, a giving, loving, warm flirting partner, really care about this man or woman. As a surprise, give this companion a phone (installation included) as a birthday, Christmas, or Valentine's present. You will receive a thank-you note from the whole family.

One other rule for becoming the consummate phone friend: Learn how to end a conversation. And do it after the first five or ten minutes. Don't linger. If someone wants to continue, let this person call you back. Five minutes of your scintillating conversation is a treat. Fifteen minutes is a chore. So have lots of fast conversations, and you'll soon need a second line to handle all the incoming calls.

**5. Learn when not to say anything.** Popularity comes from knowing when to hide feelings or desires.

## BE SLENDER

Yes, this is a tiresome reminder. If you're like lots of people, flirting makes you nervous, which in turn makes you hungry, which in turn makes you eat. And food is so closely connected with love it is hard to think of it as just body fuel. Plus, most dates revolve around eating or drinking, usually both. So what is a flirt to do?

If you really want to be absolutely the most desirable person you can be, you ought to know these statistics.

In a recent West Coast magazine which carries singles advertisements, one out of every two ads (for both men and women) suggested that the ad taker would **only** accept an encounter with someone slender. Most ads are costly and thus short. And even in this small amount of room, people felt slenderness was so crucial to romantic happiness that they listed it.

In a similar East Coast publication the ratio was one-to-three for ads placed by women, and still one-to-two for ads placed by men. Further, the ads in this eastern periodical were generally shorter, making the listing of any preference of utmost concern.

What if you'll never be model-thin? Or have anything but heavy thighs or a middle-age paunch? Then don't try to flirt in places where physical attractiveness is most flaunted. You'll do better in a quiet downtown hotel lobby than in the bar of a beach hotel. Emphasize your good qualities. You'll want to go to places and events where interest, knowledge, or ability count most. You'll do far better at a computer seminar if you know something about computer circuitry, than at an aerobics class.

Wherever you go, make sure to dress in a way that minimizes your physical flaws and maximizes your physical assets. Wear something that matches your spectacular green eyes or shows off your shapely calf or powerful muscles.

People who consider themselves heavy usually feel most attractive at night. Maybe they feel the darkness hides pounds. It does. Or they figure many potential dating partners have night blindness. But there also appears to be an attitude change about themselves at this time of day. Very heavy nightclub singers and charismatic speakers who are overweight tend to draw their biggest crowds late in the evening. So show up at a cocktail party at 10:00 P.M. instead of 8:00. Take a nap before 9:00 P.M., and then go to a movie. You may not lose weight, but you'll gain flirting confidence from these nighttime outings.

Here's one alternative dieting plan. Everytime you head for the supermarket or the take-out counter, plan on flirting three times before you get there. The response may convince you to forget that double order of pizza. After all, if you have this much luck while overweight, you could own the world when thin.

Avoid the "pretty face" or the "nice personality" trap. Or the idea that you want to be liked for yourself. Who doesn't? But take the example of Santa Claus. A nice man. Friendly, cheerful, but no question about it—a fatty! To win acceptance, he has to spend all year working on gifts for Christmas eve. And always busy flying round the world on a holiday. Even the Pritikin diet would be easier than that.

## HAVE A SENSE OF HUMOR ABOUT YOURSELF

When you are flirting, it very often feels like it's you against the world. For by flirting, you are attempting to enter a new social circle, albeit a social circle of just one person, and this can be interpreted as an intrusion. To dissipate his own anxiety or uncertainty, your potential flirting partner may engage in what fraternities and sororities call *hazing*. He may check you out by verbally sparring with you. These remarks, critiques, or asides are not to be taken seriously; never put yourself down! This teasing should be taken with a grain of salt, and will give you a chance to enter the group. So allow this to go on a bit in the initial phases of flirting, and you'll succeed with people others have called unapproachable or unfriendly.

Before you rule out this man because of his insensitivity, remember his behavior shows that he is fearful of new encounters. He needs a group. Get him away from this gang, and he is putty. Realize that this need makes him more receptive to you in the long run than someone who is more socially secure.

## BE PLAYFUL

Flirting is child's play. It is putting the childlike qualities of love, life, and romance back into life. If you're feeling terribly serious or angry or stubborn, you can't flirt. But should you get the urge to do something slightly silly, you are in the most inspired of moods for flirting.

Don't take flirting seriously. After all, you're just testing the romantic waters; you're not diving in.

With this spirit, you'll succeed in bringing out your own childlike candor as well as that of a new companion. So be casual and whimsical and prankish. Imagine yourself at a birthday party when you were eight. Think of the fun you had at summer camp when all the counselors got drunk. Then try to recreate that joie de vivre, and you'll magnify your allure.

To flirt, you've got to dredge up the little boy or girl inside you, the one who's been neglected by your drive for success.

And when you discover that four- or five-year-old, give that person some freedom. For in flirting you can safely exhibit your untapped spontaneity. And very successful flirts can not only unearth their own childlike sense, but can bring it out in someone else. Should you accomplish this, you'll create a bond that will be special, unduplicable, and definitely flirtatious.

## PERSIST

Persistence pays off. Of course you won't persist like a clod. You won't even let anyone know you *are* persisting. But you'll continue. You'll keep that certain someone high on your flirting agenda, and you'll do it in a way that makes him feel attractive. But he won't know that, he'll simply think of you as someone really nice.

And you won't give up when he announces he's in love. Or when she comes in and starts telling the entire office about her fabulous weekend. You'll put on blinders. Oh, you won't start an IRA account in her name, or put him in your will. But along with the dozens of other people you like, and flirt with, this person will be on your standard menu.

Here's why: I have a friend who is on one of the top-rated series in television. She is the star. And, because of her visibility and her interest in political and social happenings, she gets to meet everyone. Well, "S." was semi-engaged for the longest time to a very influential person. So the men who swarmed around her earlier lost hope. When S. realized her current "intended" was not Mr. Right, she quietly slipped the engagement ring she had hidden from Joan Rivers off her finger. But, by that time she had discouraged so many prospective suitors that for a time she simply gave up dating. So, when she first met Roger skiing, she liked him, but gave him only her office phone number, knowing that it was impossible to get through to her there. But Roger didn't give up. He telephoned and telephoned. He sent flowers. He sent notes. He sent a limo. And then he started calling again. When S. finally decided to see him for a quick drink, Roger asked her to marry him. When S. saw him again for another quick drink, he asked again. Now, I'm not fooling when I say that within two months S. was engaged again, and last winter, she tied the knot. Honest.

Obviously her new husband was nice and kind and fun to be with, but was that reason enough for marrying a man? No. S. said she married him because he was so persistent.

## SHOW YOUR VULNERABILITY

Vulnerability is one of the most critically important assets any flirt can possess. That's because when you flirt you are the aggressor. You've selected the man or woman you'd like to deal with. You've decided when to act. You're in control. But when you tame this flirting power with vulnerability, your flirting partner will find you exquisitely approachable.

Why is Snoopy far more appealing and loveable than those Barbie dolls? No, it isn't the fact that he is nude. It's his defenselessness.

Showing vulnerability means revealing little insecurities in a way that makes them seem like positive assets.

Are you afraid of the dark, snakes, the Russians, or the I.R.S.? Think about it. Do you think that jobs are getting scarce? Discuss this. Reveal the real, more tender side of you, but don't open yourself up for hurt. Select your revelations intelligently.

Consider your flaws. Which of them can be turned into flirting assets? Are you uncomfortable with large groups? Say so. Do you procrastinate? Tell him he'll either have millions of suggestions on how to help or admit he shares your foible.

Uneasy with math, computers, children, crabgrass, flying, overtime, unions, politics? A helpmate will soon rush to fill this abyss of knowledge or to placate your anxiety. Either way, you'll both start feeling more comfortable, more loving, and more flirtatious.

## FLIRT WITH NO EXPECTATION OF REWARD

"What!" you say, "How ridiculous!" That's right. The ridiculous, the miraculous, and the emotional, all play a part in flirting. To expect a flirtation to end in marriage, a new job, or a ride home takes the innocence out of this social interaction.

To flirt well, you must assume that the pleasure you get from flirting is an end in itself. Of course, flirting can lead to just about anything. But the purity of your flirting motives is what will carry your flirtation off in style.

By psyching yourself up to expect anything other than a brief affirmation of how desirable you are, you are asking for trouble. Because then flirting becomes a means to an end. To get all the secondary benefits of flirting, you must not think about them, because the mere act of trying to imagine where something might lead usually stops it dead in its tracks.

Flirting is much like a good joke. Just as a good joke depends on the element of surprise, so flirting surprises both the person you have chosen to flirt with—and you. Think of flirting in the same way you think about the Wanted posters at the post office. You are there just to buy stamps, not to catch one of the Ten Most Wanted Criminals. Should you see one of the faces from the mug shots, you point it out to the police; but you aren't counting on that reward money to pay next month's rent. However, you *will* leave the police with your name and number in case the criminal is apprehended. The same thing you'd give to a flirting partner.

## HAVE SIMULTANEOUS FLIRTING OBJECTIVES

You know what a nervous wreck you can become when you're waiting for just one person to call? Or, if you're happiness depends on one woman, how anxious you are around her? Even in business, if the bottom line depends on one customer, you can't act normally with that one client as you would act with your smaller accounts.

So to be a really great flirt, you must spread your risk around, as they say in the investment business. Never leave home with only one flirting objective. Oh, of course, it may be most important to get Jane to agree to a date with you, but make sure you want to see Cindy and Lori and Debbie too. Because people sense panic. And there is nothing more conducive to panic than a no-choice situation.

When you get to a party or a place where you might engage in a bit of flirting, never, ever, select just one person to flirt with. Select four or five. Even if you are flirting in the grocery store or the bank, don't stop with one; make sure you engage in a handful of tiny flirtations. Why do you think Maid Marian kept all those merry men around?

If you don't meet enough people in one day to have multiple

encounters, don't judge your flirting on a day-to-day basis. Judge it weekly. However, make this promise to yourself: If you flirt even once, you'll flirt a minimum of five or six other times that day, or at least that week.

## STAY FLEXIBLE

Part of the fun of flirting is knowing that anything can happen. You may find love, you may find adventure, and you may taste unusual delights. But you won't experience any of these pleasures if you stay stuck in your current mind-set.

You must stay flexible if you want all the benefits of flirting. Is it going to kill you to taste pistachio ice cream when your favorite is mocha almond? What's so bad about listening to Greek music for three hours, even if it's not your favorite? Flirting will introduce you to far more new interests, people, and lifestyles than you'd ever get sticking to the tried and true.

Flexibility means sharing. If you meet a man who's everything your mother wanted you to marry, but who reminds you too much of your ex-husband, show your good will by introducing him to your sister.

Being flexible allows you to recognize when something isn't working, and to admit it immediately. So you joined a gourmet cooking class to meet women, and every classmate is a man? Get out of there fast. Don't stick around where you know you're not wanted or where you are bored. Move on.

When you flirt, everything seems momentarily possible. A new man doesn't like to scuba dive? Don't worry, next week's flirting partner may be an aqua-nut.

And there is nothing that keeps you younger than the ability to adapt to new circumstances. When you lose that urge to rearrange the furniture in a partner's apartment, or you no longer notice when your girl friend cuts her long hair off, your flexibility, youthfulness, and passion are in a state of remission. Rush to the nearest flirting hot spot; you are in desperate need of a romantic transfusion.

## LEARN TO DANCE

Do it. Assuming you'll pick up a few basic steps while at a charity ball isn't enough. You need to know the basics and then some. And having gone to dancing school when you were an adolescent doesn't count.

For both men and women dancing has lots of advantages. Both women and men look sensual when dancing slow, and very sexy when doing the newest dances, all of which are blatant advertisements for a beautiful body. But even if you lack perfect proportions, dancing brings out your creativity; you become more romantic, and the emotional side of you is unleashed.

There is nothing more flirtatious than dancing with a new partner. And the great thing about dancing, is that it can serve a dual purpose for serious flirts. While you are dancing with one person, the way you move, the ease with which you move your body, are all signals to potential flirting partners who are watching. And a flirtatious glance to a new acquaintance, while you are performing your terpsichorean talents with another, could be a potent flirting signal.

## SHOW ENTHUSIASM FOR THE MOMENT

Intensify your reactions. If you are at a party, appear as if it's the best one you've ever attended. If you are at a bar, notice the decor or lack of it. You needn't be pleased with your setting, although this will endear you to a person (what person wants the place he has chosen to go to criticized?), but you do need to be dramatic. If some place, food, decor, party, evening, service, work, or experience is really dreadful, make it the *most* awful thing. Go in one direction or the other. If you act dynamically, others may. If you don't, you may have another evening down the drain.

Be optimistic about how the event might go. Don't appear negative. Be intensely interested in it. Opinions evoke discussions — and that's the point of this whole thing anyway, right?

## SURROUND YOURSELF WITH LAUGHTER

You don't want to be a stand-up comic, but it sure boosts an evening if someone can be funny. While making yourself the butt of jokes makes you the center of attention, it is lonely attention. Who can really enjoy being put down? And what confident human being would be attracted to someone who constantly puts themselves down and allows others to?

Therefore, if you want to eat your cake and have it too, prepare ahead of time to be amusing. Not funny, amusing. Carry a funny cartoon. Have a funny story or joke ready. What, you don't know any?

Do what the experts do. Subscribe to a comedy newsletter, where you can get current one-liner jokes even before the disc jockeys use them on the radio. Cut out an amusing story from *Reader's Digest* and memorize it. Do keep all jokes and anecdotes short. Then if something goes wrong, so what? Don't build up a story before telling it. Just do it. And finally, if a joke dies, or no one laughs, ask that person to tell a joke or funny story of her own. In other words, don't stop because you get a bad reaction. If Woody Allen had done this, he'd have never filmed *Zelig* after doing *A Midsummer Night's Sex Comedy*.

## GET OUT OF A WIN/LOSE MENTALITY

Flirting is a game, but it is a game without scoring. No matter what those sex magazines might imply. Scoring, judging, criticizing, and especially one-upping all go strongly against the grain of any sincere flirt.

To flirt is to test, cajole, play, try out, and to enjoy. Flirting is non-judgmental. And good flirting has Zen-like qualities. Flirting is an end in itself. Simply by doing it, you have accomplished, perfectly, what you set out to do.

It may not be true in sports, but in flirting it's not winning or losing but how you play the game that counts.

## VISUALIZE YOURSELF FLIRTING

Without a good, clear image of yourself as a successful flirt, you probably won't ever reach the heights of great flirting.

Lacking a precise image of what a flirt is, you succumb to your old, limiting picture of yourself as a rather staid person.

To flirt you must give yourself permission to dream about the marvelous outcome of a flirtatious evening. You must see yourself, in your mind's eye, doing the town and being congratulated for your panache and sparkling personality.

This visualization may be hard because in the back of your head, you may equate a flirt with someone who is promiscuous or insincere. You may not want to be called a flirt. All right. Call flirting anything you want. Call it socializing. Call it relating. Call it meeting new people. Then visualize how you'd like your next flirtatious encounter to go. Don't go further than flirting. But do picture the following:

♡————————————————————————♡

**Visualization #1:** Picture yourself flirting at work. You not only have done a brilliant job, but the most attractive single man, or woman, in your company comes over to talk with you about further projects you can do together. What happens next . . .

**Visualization #2:** You are shopping, and suddenly you see someone you liked once before, but haven't seen in years. He is carrying lots of packages, or she is rushed but weary enough to join you for coffee. What do you do . . .

**Visualization #3:** You are on vacation. No one is around, but then you see the most perfect body coming out of the water and onto the sand. You realize this person is coming in your direction. How do you act . . .

**Visualization #4:** It is a boring, routine day. The telephone rings and it is an old friend who wants to see you again. Where and when do you meet . . .

**Visualization #5:** You are ending an unhappy romance or marriage. You decide to go on a long trip to a favorite resort or a dreamt-about destination. You discover that your seat mate, who's of the opposite sex, is also in similar circumstances. How do you encourage this new aquaintance . . .

**Visualization #6:** Your best friend and your worst enemy have both gotten married, and you are sick to death of hearing this news, because you feel so alone. You go to the wedding of your best friend, and meet someone very special. How do you spend the rest of your time at the wedding reception . . .

**Visualization #7:** You have just finished playing the best set of tennis, the best game of golf, or the best racquetball, done the most push-ups, the most artistic dance workout, the longest run, or the most impressive work project, or won an election, contest, prize or honor. As you are being applauded and congratulated on your personal success, an elegant man or woman comes over to you, shakes your hand and asks you how you did it? What are your next romantic moves . . .

## KEEP A JOURNAL

Boswell did it, Wall Street does it, and pilots do it for the F.A.A. If flirting and romance are important to you, you should keep a journal too. This is not documentation for a romantic novel. It's purely for anthropological purposes. And to find out what works.

Why chronicle failures, disappointments, and even semi-successes? To improve.

The most effective way to do this is to keep a "Flirting Journal." Before you think of how tedious this must be, let me point out that this is not your normal page-after-page journal. Since it deals with short encounters, it only requires short entries. And before you dismiss this idea, realize that this journal can cut the time you **waste** flirting almost in half within a week. And if you keep at this for a mere twenty-one days, you'll find a 300 percent increase in effectiveness. And twenty-one entries isn't hard, is it?

When you are flirting, you find out so many things about yourself. You may realize that you like women who are first very cold, because you like to see them warm up just for you. Or you may notice that you flirt best when you have a date all planned for the next evening. Or after one man approaches you and flirts with you, your flirting style may become more flamboyant, open, or positive. Or a man you feel you have "won" away from another woman, may seem overwhelmingly attractive to you solely for that reason.

These minor quirks illuminate a great deal about how you respond in all male/female relationships. If you like someone who's initially cold (as in the above example), you may subconsciously attract a male or female partner who requires that you bring most of the love and nurturing to the relationship. Should you feel most drawn to a man you have to lure from another woman, you may find that you choose to love a man who is constantly making you jealous. Because when he appears to like another woman, you can rewin his affection. These flirting patterns are not once-in-a-blue-moon occurrences. They are so symptomatic of what happens in long-term liaisons that you can learn a great deal about your committed relationships, as well as improving and perfecting your flirting style, by incorporating these observations into your flirting routine.

Certain gestures, actions, words, looks, touches, and places will bring out the best in you. Which ones are they? You'll only learn from trial and error. But if you don't write down the triumphs, the mistakes, the fabulous and the awful times you've had, they may all fade into a mere impression of what happened. It is the tiny, unmemorable specifics that make or break a flirtatious gesture. So put it down in your Flirting Journal.

First impressions count. Your own and that of others. Here's a secret that one flirting expert learned from keeping a Flirting Journal. Joanna wanted to get married. Her objective in flirting was to bring new men into her life, in order to find someone to marry. Joanna kept her little Flirting Journal, but she went one step further. She put down how a man treated her on their first date. (Did he ask her which movie she'd like to go to? Did he monopolize the conversation? Did he get overly familiar? Was he on time? Was he kind to her dog? Did he see her to the door? And then, did he call her the next day? Was he overly wrapped up in his work? Overly impressed with her material possessions? A heavy drinker?) Joanna made notes after every date. In fact, the more she liked a man, and was under his spell, the more she noted every little fact—good, bad, and neutral.

Her Flirting Journal proved invaluable when any of her relationships started going sour. Before keeping a journal, she would have blamed herself for not being more loving or attractive when a relationship didn't work out. But with her Flirting Journal, she would go over her *early notes*—the most revealing part of any analysis. And those first impressions usually proved to be, *not* overly critical, but essentially accurate. When the romance got bumpy, Joanna could assess how much, or how little, she contributed to a man's negative behavior. And it was very helpful when she had reached the commitment stage and found out he hadn't.

So Joanna, who wanted to flirt because she was 100 percent marriage-minded, began heeding those first ominous signals. She would ease herself out of a budding relationship with a man whose actions seemed unacceptable in the long run. And she saved herself a great deal of time. Joanna weeded out the people who weren't for her on the first date or two, and went merrily along searching for Mr. Right. She found him and married him, all within six months. And Joanna didn't have the easiest time of it, because she just happens to be blind.

For those who want only to flirt casually, you may not scrutinize a flirting companion with as much specificity. After all, if you are just flirting you don't care if he doesn't like your family. Of if she doesn't call you when she says she will, or refuses to give you an answer about a date until 4 P.M. on a Saturday afternoon. But by recognizing your own flirting style, and what type of person you get the most flirting pleasure from, you put your flirtatious moments to best use.

# ♡ III ♡
# HOW TO FLIRT

# ♡ 13 ♡
# *20 Ways to Be a Great Flirt*

BECAUSE FLIRTING REQUIRES A CAREFREE HEART, IT IS ESSENTIAL THAT YOU BEGIN YOUR FLIRTATIONS WITH MODEST EXPECTATIONS. This has multiple benefits: You are more likely to have small triumphs at the beginning, which will encourage you to continue. You have less invested in flirting, thereby making you more discriminating about when and with whom you flirt. And you'll have fewer initial mistakes, particularly the most common error, that of overdoing. In fact, a good rule of thumb is to follow what television and film actors do when they get nervous

A SMALL TRIUMPH

over a performance. They do *less* not more, realizing that their inner, pent-up energies will give more punch than they intend to their lines and gestures.

## 1.   Use Flattery

Flattery, if combined with the three basics of flirting (see Chapter 3), is to flirting what a match is to dynamite. Explosive. So to refine the power of flattery, you must be sincere. Keep in mind that not only must *you* think a person looks good tonight, he must in some way think he does too.

Expert, successful, mutually rewarding flattery is much harder to pull off than anyone thinks. Here are some guidelines:

**a.** Figure out what strikes you about this person. (There probably will be several things.)

**b.** Which of these potentially flattering statements would he most like to hear from someone else? What area of his person, accomplishments, or activities have not been totally confirmed by society?

**c.** Once you have determined this, use it.

*Example*: It is well known that beautiful women hear how pretty they look, time and time again. Why, I thought, would a gorgeous woman not want this reaffirmed? The answer is they *do* want it reaffirmed, but in a way that shows a man has really looked. Most of the compliments they receive are common, ordinary, unimaginative statements about their appearance. This leaves them with the old nagging suspicion that they are being fed a line.

Sarah told me this, "I hear the standard, 'You're so pretty, you're so beautiful,' so often from men, and even when it is inappropriate, that I often think they haven't even looked at me that day, that they're doing this by rote. I want to hear—if it's true—that a dress fits me perfectly (I go to a lot of trouble to look good, you know), or that I look good enough for a magazine

"You smell as good as you look."

cover, or that I look very sexy. What I'd like from a complimentary remark is to know that someone went to the trouble of thinking about me as an individual, instead of just hearing the same old lines."

Flattery is most effective when there is an element of surprise. When someone doesn't expect the compliment. Telling a football player that he is "exciting to watch on the playing field" is nice. But saying that you "love his sense of humor and his smile" will make his day. The first compliment he knows himself, the second he may suspect, but the fact that you mentioned this is delightful and surprising.

## 2.  Say Hello with Energy

When you say hello, pretend that there is an electrical current pulsating through your body. It is brief—like turning on a light bulb just for a second. Remember that what follows from an introduction or meeting depends on how your new acquaintance perceives your hello. Practice it. Listen to your voice on a tape recorder. Does it sound like you are happy to see him? Or does your tone project boredom, lack of interest, low energy, anxiety, or fear. Put a little sparkle in your voice, a lilt; but keep the overall pitch low.

## 3.  Shake Hands

Handshakes are too formal for people interested in flirting, you think? Think again. Reaching out, touching a hand, holding it, squeezing it, and letting go are all very sensual, tactile, personal activities. When else, unless you make it to the hand-holding stage, will you hold this person's hand again? Probably not until you shake hands good-bye, but after that, never! Hand-holding, touching, and caressing are practiced either between complete strangers or intimates. Why not for those in between? Because hands are one of the most sensitive parts of the body. During the intermediate stages of a relationship, hands project too much sensuality. So make your first handshake count.

What to do? Make your handshakes memorable. Don't prove what a tough, confident man or woman you are by crushing the

(WRONG)

(RIGHT)

other person's fingers. If you notice rings on a hand, be especially careful, for a handshake with a twisted ring can be excruciating and shows very little finesse, sensitivity, or concern for others. Stay away from the limp handshake too. You want him to know he's holding a hand, not a dead fish.

As in saying hello, a handshake needs special energy. Before you shake hands, mentally dwell on the sensations you expect to feel and receive in your right hand and arm. Focus attention to that spot, put energy into it, but not strength. Try these:

**Flirtatious Handshake #1—The Politician:** In this handshake you reach out with your right hand. If you are a woman, you should then reach out and slightly brush the fingers of his right hand with your left hand. This must be done quickly, so it's barely noticed. If you are a man, with your left hand touch either her wrist, the top of her right hand, or the fingers on her right hand. If both of you reach out with your left hands, don't panic, you can each confess that you read this book.

This handshake got its name from politicians who must shake hands with bone-crushers. The politician grabs the voter's wrist so tightly that the surprised voter loosens his grasp. (Also, the wrist maneuver can take the emphasis off the right hand, saving the politician for the next crowd.) When used for business, this handshake can either seem very sincere or a bit too hearty. Test it a few times on your dad before you try it on the boss.

**Flirtatious Handshake #2—The Squeeze:** While The Politician can be used in business, The Squeeze is far too subtle and sexual for that. At the end of the shake, you finish with a tiny, extra squeeze. This should not be tight but merely a surge of energy. Then let go. Doing this signals that you are warm, confident, and something more than just pleased to meet someone—you are indicating there is a definite attraction.

## 4. Make Immediate, Direct Eye Contact

If coordinated with what you are saying, this is the most effective and direct flirting technique. And even when not coordinated, it can be dazzling. Eye contact establishes intimacy: it can be either intrusive or caring. So the power with which you lock eyes for the first time will determine the starting level of the conversation. If you lock eyes in a tentative fashion, expect a tentative conversation. If you feel a thunderbolt, fantastic! But watch out—overly sexual or inviting eye invitations are the main cause of misinterpretations of motives between two people. So when using thunderbolt eye contact, make sure you're really ready for an "electrical" evening—don't be "shocked" by anything that happens.

## 5. Repeat the Person's Name

Follow the three-times rule regarding names. Repeat the name when you are introduced. "John?!? Great to meet you." Do it again when talking to your flirting partner or when referring to her in a three-way conversation. And mention it a third time when saying good-bye.

You can increase your chances of flirting success by doing your new companion a favor. Remind him of *your name*. Include it in an anecdote you are telling. This is not your egomaniacal streak coming out (although egomaniacs will do this more than necessary). Your flirting partner may be as bad with names as you once were. (A thing of the past, isn't it?) He may not have caught the correct pronunciation. Introductions are anxious moments, and rather than admit that she isn't sure if it's Joe or Josh, a woman may spend her time thinking of how she can catch a glimpse of your name on your credit cards. This diverts your partner's attention, making it difficult to establish any rapport. Plus, if someone doesn't know your name, they have nothing to attach to the telephone number you may have given them.

## 6. Ask "No One Ever Asked Me That Before" Questions

People are always interested in themselves. In fact, one definition of love is, "What another person feels toward you when you reflect for them a view of what they'd like to think they are." The same holds true in flirting, only on a more fundamental level. Each person loves to have someone as interested in him as he is himself. One way to satisfy that common desire is to ask questions. Not overly personal questions, but questions which are uncommon.

I have a male friend who had no luck with women at all. He was 5'5", 300 pounds, not very charming or gracious, but very, very smart. Suddenly I saw the most attractive women with him. How did his happen? I wondered. He told me his magical secret.

"I just ask women the questions that no one has ever asked them before. I figure out where they are in their lives, I think about what they probably are thinking about, and then I ask them questions about their life goals, about their basic beliefs, and about what they want from a relationship. Almost overnight it worked. I even changed my home telephone number because one woman kept hounding me."

What would happen if some other man started asking those questions?

"I'd just figure out the next question that he didn't ask. You can tell when you hit that question, the one no one has asked, because the women become fountains of information gushing forth. No one ever talks about these important issues. Now I find it hard getting rid of these women, because they all say I know them better than anyone ever did."

## 7. Do a Double Take

Have you noticed that people can tell when you are staring at them even in a car? How they turn and stare back? A double take has the effect of staring, but is 100 percent better. In effect, you are saying that something (another person, object, or activity) caught your attention. Since humans are by nature curious, this person will want to know what you see. She will meet your gaze, and—Eureka!—from across a crowded room something will have begun.

It takes time to perfect a double take, but here's how. A double take is a fast turn of the head to one side, then a turn back, and thirdly a fast, exaggerated turn back to that same one side, where you stay for ten seconds or more.

## 8. Ask for Your New Friend's Life Story

Everyone *loves* to talk about themselves—and after they've revealed some of their inner thoughts and ambitions, they feel *so* close to you. A magical bond has been established. But the trick here is to go first. If you ask a person out of the blue to tell you about themselves, it amounts to a demand to perform and puts them on the defensive. (What does he want to know *this* for? Or, is she from the credit bureau?) But if you go first, they'll feel much more open and will reveal more.

Carefully choose the place for all this. Are there people around who can hear? Then don't exchange life stories. Few people want to tell you intimate details about themselves while standing in line for a movie, surrounded by loads of people.

## 9. Have Something to Say by Keeping Up-to-Date

One of the pluses of being with another person is that you are stimulated intellectually. Another person makes you think of things, do things, try things, and vicariously experience things you normally wouldn't. So, make sure you are a good partner when you flirt. The easiest, fastest, and best way to keep up to date is to familiarize yourself with the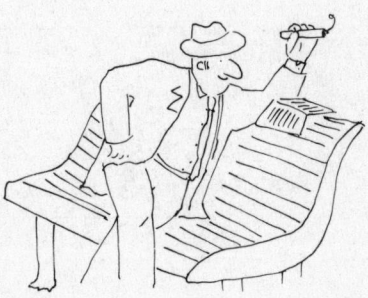

"Best" or "Top" lists. They include: best-selling books, records, videos; top-grossing movies; et cetera. Keep your ears open for literary, theatrical, artistic, and scientific awards. Find out the top TV shows (I know *you* don't watch them, but someone does), investigate the top companies in one of the fields that fascinate you. If you want to find out about the past year, the *World Almanac* is a godsend. But for the up-to-the-minute information that's going to impress others this weekend, try a weekly newsmagazine—although the most impressive sources are trade journals that tell you the most commercially and artistically successful new ventures.

## 10.  *Play with a Piece of Clothing*

*For women:* Dangle a shoe in a rhythmic way, play with an earring. Applying a tiny bit of lip gloss from a pot can be very flirtatious, but avoid powdering your nose, it makes you look old. The secret here is not in what you are doing, but in the rhythmic movements you are making. Rhythm is very sexual, it is also very comforting. Like the rocking of a chair, the ocean, or a hammock. By duplicating these careful, non-urgent activity patterns, you set up a siren call to men.

*For men:* Adjust your tie, your cuffs, your hair. Twirl your drink. Pacing is very masculine, and if done in a steady tempo can be somewhat appealing. It also allows a woman to ask why you are doing that. Other rhythmic activities are driving around the block in a car, playing basketball by yourself (a ball bouncing is very rhythmic), or playing pinball.

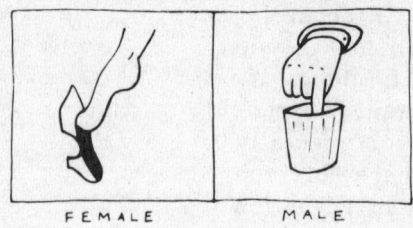

FEMALE        MALE

## 11. To Get Subtle Attention—Whisper

Dressing, shouting, or coming in and telling a man, "I think I just hit your car," will get an immediate response. But they won't bring an immediate *positive* response. What will? **Whispering.**

When you were little, you were told not to whisper. It wasn't polite to exclude. But not all whispering is rude, sometimes it's an intimate flirting technique.

Should you want to get the attention of someone across the room, try whispering into someone else's ear close to you. It will make others wonder, "Why is she excluding me?" or think, "What is that man saying about me to his friend?" Whispers invoke fear and intrigue, and make people want to be included.

You do need a partner for this technique, preferably one of the same sex, if you have your eye on another person. Now face in her direction but whisper in the ear of a friend. Now smile at her. You'll certainly get her attention. If she's close, she may even approach you.

Once you have started a conversation with your intended, you can still use this potent force. When talking to him, whisper. Now, try whispering (it doesn't matter what) in his ear. This has very potent sexual overtones. Don't do it unless you are sure you like him, as it is easy to lead him on doing this. For men, whispering is a gentle thing. In connotes to a woman that she is worthy of confiding in, even if you are talking about the Washington Redskins.

For a woman, whispering is very helpful in making that difficult transformation from competent, daytime executive to feminine nighttime woman. If you prefer not to be an authority figure in your personal life, and have a hard time shifting gears quickly, make a conscious decision to whisper in order to ease this transition.

## 12. Help Someone Get Out of an Old Routine, and Into a New One

We are all creatures of habit. Some of them are good, some bad, but most of them are just routines that make life simpler. And boring. If you can help someone out of an old routine and into a new one, you automatically become an integral part of the new ritual in that person's mind. For instance, if you encourage someone you've had your eye on for a long time to jog with you, it will be hard for her to think of jogging without remembering how the two of you did it together. Playing tennis always reminds someone of other partners. Participating in any new hobby or activity is good, but doing something new that's physical creates an indelible impression. And a good one. Think back to the first person you played chopsticks with. Don't you remember him?

Introduce her to the joys of Bergman, and she'll never see *The Seventh Seal* without remembering you. Teach him chess and . . . well, who else can he play with? Show him how to do back exercises. All right, you break up with him. But then his back goes out. Doesn't he wish you were still around him?

One of the pleasures of flirting or responding to flirting is in the new adventure that awaits you. Whether for a moment, or an evening, or a lifetime. (What, you've *never* been sailing or on a roller coaster or to a high-tech furniture showroom?)

But the flirt who becomes ingrained in someone's daily routine, has something else going for him: his flirting power carries over to the activity itself. And much like a television rerun, every time the new routine is followed, he gets a residual—she thinks of him.

## 13. Leave Them Wanting More

In show business, politics, and sports, the pros leave the crowd shouting for more. Even Johnny Carson. After all, he did cut back his TV show to one hour—and we want more.

And the national news. We ought to have an hour of national news on one network, other than PBS. But do we? No. The researchers say that people will then have *too* much news, better to "Leave them wanting more."

THE OLDEST TRICK IN THE BOOK

When you flirt, you are giving someone your undivided attention. There is nothing more flattering. However, people want what it appears they cannot have. An expert flirt will emote until the man she is trying to attract responds. Then she will back off. When things are going well, a good flirt won't wait around until the conversation hits a bump. She will leave.

So, follow the successful flirts. Leave the second you know you're hitting off fabulously with someone *and* you're sure you'll see or hear from him again. Or you're sure you can make this chance encounter recur. Don't let him move on to new conquests before you do. Don't try to improve the situation; save that for the next time. By staying too long, you lose your mystery, your power, and a bit of your allure. Prolong the pleasure.

The ancients knew this. Even in arranged marriages the parents knew that if the bride and groom saw too much of each other *before* the wedding, one might back out.

## 14.   Create and Use Nicknames

When you observe happy couples, you'll notice that they call each other by special pet names—reserved to them alone.

The use and creation of nicknames can precede or follow new relationships, but it is a very important stepping-stone to intimacy. Nicknames are fun; there's a childlike, spontaneous quality to them, and an underlying knowledge that they mean a bit more than the name implies. Plus, nicknames make everyone else seem like an outsider.

So as soon as you can find a clever nickname to call someone, do. It can be a short phrase, but one or two short words is best. And make sure the other person creates one for you. Normally

this will happen as a basic outgrowth of fumbling around to get to know each other. Does he like Lite Beer? Are you a pistachio-nut freak?

The name must not be too common or too flattering, and never mean. It should be based on a private aspiration, dream, interest, or revelation. A simple guide: Imagine you are calling this flirting partner, person-to-person long distance, collect. Could they discern strictly from the way you refer to them, that it is *you* calling? If so, your pet name is right on the money.


## 15.   Drop Names

Yes. Some people will think this a social gaffe. Should they remind you of this, tell them that Emily Post never lived in the eighties.

Why drop names? Because names are our connection to a society. Everything is named: your street, brand of car, this book, airlines, even your favorite soft drink has a name. Names bring us closer to each other and to things. They personalize even dry conversations. Notice how the phone company representative gives a name before telling you your service is about to be suspended.

But when you are flirting, names give you cachet and credibility, and add to your social profile. Plus, people like to feel connected to you in some way. If the gorgeous brunette just happens to work with your friend Jennifer, tell her so. Tell a man you're flirtatiously talking to that you once interviewed for a job at the firm where he works. ("With whom?" he will ask.) This is the connective tissue of social interchange.

At a party, both of you must know the host or hostess in some way. That is a perfect start. If you are waiting for a plane, mention your travel agent. And what if you don't know anyone your new friend does? You both might have used the same bank, or written to the same Congressman, or been stranded at O'Hare (everyone has been) one winter.  From these seemingly bland experiences springs a connection. And this connection makes your flirting partner more willing to let down his guard about other facets of his life.

The names you drop needn't be social or famous or important. You aren't trying to get a loan from this person or to impress her with your pseudo-importance, you're trying to find common ground. In fact, sprinkling your conversation with phony references to your close friendship with Dolly Parton, may make your partner feel alienated or so out of your social sphere that you lose out.

For male flirts, dropping names of local heros, dignitaries, or well-known people in the community can be quite helpful with a woman. Because no matter how frivolous a woman, in the back of her mind she is mentally gauging if you are "dangerous" or "threatening" to her. By giving a woman some proof of your stability, you enhance your attractiveness, because she no longer has to deal with the little voice in her head, warning her to "Watch Out."

## 16. Wear, Bring, or Carry Something Unusual

In decorating, this would be called a conversation piece. When you were little, it was that monstrosity on the coffee table that elicited questions whenever it was hauled out. Then your mother would go into her story about how she discovered this treasure, and your father, at a garage sale. In the seventies, the T-shirt served this purpose. Then in the late seventies it was the bumper sticker. But now that novelties no longer seem interesting or personal, you have to invent or acquire your own conversation starters. It can be a piece of clothing, jewelry that is more outrageous than pretty, a book you carry, a jigsaw puzzle you bring with you, your hat, or any personal quirk.

Once you have this invaluable item, if people don't ask you questions about it, you can use this object to begin conversations. Ask people to help you with this "thing." They will just because they've been dying to find out more about it. The fact that you are discussing not you or them, but your *object*, makes the flirting so much more discreet, and effective.

WOULD YOU MIND HELPING ME WITH THIS THING?

## 17. Use the Old 1 – 2 – 3 Routine

Picture a moth flirting with a flame; there's a dance in and out. Duplicate this for the 1 – 2 – 3 flirting technique. Your boldest move is the first one. It is the time you are as assertive as you are ever going to be. The "1" is your approach. It is dazzling, outrageous, flirtatious, bold, appealing, overly forward, and spontaneous.

The "2" is a complete back-off. After two or three minutes of displaying your delightful personality, back off. Distance yourself from your flirting companion. You might leave to get a new drink, you might put on a sweater, you might say hello to a friend, you might tie your jogging shoe, you could search for your car keys. Anything, so long as the focus is totally off the formally flirtatious behavior. This gives your partner a chance to assess you. Not to scrutinize, but to take in your presence. If there is too much of a rush about you, it not only seems too forward, but also threatening and undesirable.

Now during phase 2, you don't back off totally. Keep in non-verbal contact. It's like riding in a car with someone you know very well. You needn't talk all the time. Those quiet periods don't mean that you don't care for someone; it just means you are comfortable. That's the feeling to try to duplicate in this couple of minutes.

The "3" is a renewal of flirting. But not to the degree of the initial flirtation. The best guideline is about 80 percent of your original intensity. Continue between 60 and 80 percent for the rest of the time you are with someone. And, as the time together progresses, you might even tone that down to 40 or 50 percent. By this time, your flirting partner will be contributing to some of the flirting, and if he isn't maybe it's time to move on. In flirting and baseball, three strikes and you're out.

## 18. Try Intermittent Reinforcement

Studies have shown that the most effective way to get someone to do something consistently, is not to give them constant praise or constant criticism, but to *intermittently* give rewards.

This is equally effective when flirting. Think back. A man flirts with you for a while, and then pays *no attention* to you at all. Don't you think you did something wrong? (Did he see the run in your stocking?)

This is intermittent reinforcement working overtime. And this is a fabulous—albeit a bit calculating—technique for making someone start worrying about your opinion.

Remember the man who waited three days to call you after you and he decided to spend Christmas together? Of course you do. Those three days of hell when it was all you could do not to call him at the office?

Or the woman who tells a man, "Call me sometime," but never answers her phone and never returns any messages, until she's good and ready.

Intermittent reinforcement is most effective when you are going to be flirting with one person over an extended length of time. (That can be one evening, one weekend, one month.) First you must give an extraordinary amount of attention to this person. You must think he is brilliant, totally fascinating. Tell him. Show him. And even (oh, this isn't quite fair to tell you) tell your friends within his earshot how marvelous this new love is. Boast about this person.

Then, in the time it takes to get a parking receipt validated, go to the ladies room, or pay the tab, you move into the withdrawal phase of the reinforcement. No, you are not cold or uncaring. But you have so many *other* things on your mind. Now when he says something that is genuinely brilliant, you mention that you read that in the *Wall Street Journal*. Or when she thinks she is being fascinating by revealing her interest in architectural styles, tell her you wonder why anyone would want to improve on the basic shape of the tent.

Now don't be mean or cruel. The tone to really strike is one of **self-revelation**. That now the focus is on you. Or you might just want to project an aura of neutrality or disinterest. You now don't care if the MX missiles are deployed or not, whereas last night you were ready to enlist in the army.

You will know that you have properly executed this technique when your new flirting companion asks, "What's wrong? Is something troubling you?" The surefire tip-off that you've played this scene perfectly is, "Did I do something wrong?"

To all of which you answer, "No." He didn't do anything wrong. He simply is so interesting and fascinating that you want to further captivate him. And this is the secret method you have chosen.

WARNING: Don't do this more than once. The intermittent reinforcement tactic should only be used when you are close to desperate. It is not necessarily nice, but it does work.

## 19.　Limit the Amount of Time You Flirt

If you are afraid of flirting, but would really like to give it a try, help yourself out by limiting the amount of time you flirt in any one day. Tell yourself you're not going to flirt after 4 P.M. when you should be studying.

Give yourself a limit to the amount of time you'll devote to the opposite sex. Say, "I'll flirt for only thirty minutes on weekdays." Or flirt only on Thursday nights.

At a party where you are trying out your flirting wings, make up your mind to flirt during the first twenty minutes of the party, and then relax. You might be having so much fun that you beg and plead with yourself to go on. But now it is something you choose to do because of the positive reinforcement.

During football season, flirt during halftime. At a car wash, flirt until your car is ready. At work, flirt only at coffee breaks, or on payday, or when you get your work done early. These mini-flirting sessions allow you to control the flirting completely. You not only determine who you flirt with, but by limiting the time, you ensure that nothing really serious transpires. This lessens any risk and gives you control. (After all, *you* are the one who is going to stop the flirting.) And control gives you confidence, which in turn releases that childlike flirting quality.

Besides, flirting can become addictive. Many almost-ex-flirts are now attending Flirts Anonymous because they didn't put these early restraints on their flirting forays.

Sorry to report that Flirts Anonymous is not the success it could, or should, be. New members join all the time, but they meet someone—have a flirting relapse—and are in the middle of some new romantic passion before we even get a chance to put them on our membership rolls. One nice thing, though, at F.A. (Flirts Anonymous) we have no problem recruiting new members; in fact, to our dismay, many addicted flirts use meetings as an occasion to flirt under the aegis of our organization.

## 20. Set a Numerical Goal

Goals motivate everyone. And since we all act more positively when we have a goal, why not use this ploy when flirting?

Tell yourself you're going to flirt until three men comment on how well your gorgeous blue dress matches your eyes. Or until three women agree to have coffee with you. Or five customers smile at you.

Having a number in mind does something else. It disassociates you from a person (which is good for beginning flirts, although this eventually could harm intimacy), so you are not as threatened by the flirting encounter. For example: If you think of Judy as the most desirable woman in your neighborhood, you put yourself under needless pressure. Lift this burden by thinking of Judy—at least for one day—not as Judy, but as the fourth woman who commented on how cute your dog is. If you think of Jerry as the most brilliant MBA you've ever met, you will take his very brusque way of answering the phone as a rejection. Think of him as your eighth flirting partner of the day, and he's back to being a normal person—someone you feel comfortable with.

# ♡ 14 ♡
# *The 5 Don'ts of Flirting*

## 1. Don't depend on others to make things happen.
If you could depend on them to get things started, you wouldn't need to flirt.

## 2. Don't tease.
Offering others more than you intend to give always back-fires.

## 3. Don't cling.
Don't monopolize one person all night long. Wait for him to indicate his desire to continue being with you.

## 4. Don't dwell on flirting.
Do it and forget it. Keep your playful tone at all times.

## 5. Don't fidget.
It's annoying. You are fidgeting when you let your nervous tension out in unintentional ways. You are *not* fidgeting if you are tapping your fingers to Stevie Wonder. You are fidgeting if you tap them throughout a supposedly flirtatious conversation.

# ♡ 15 ♡
# *Flirtatious Hints from the Media*

IF THE MEDIUM IS THE MESSAGE, AS MARSHALL MC LUHAN WOULD SAY, THEN FOR PROSPECTIVE FLIRTS, THE MESSAGE THE MEDIA BRING TO US CAN BE VERY HELPFUL IN EMBELLISHING OUR FLIRTATIOUS STYLE. Look at the ads in magazines. They are the advertising world's interpretation of the most potent flirting techniques. Surprised? You shouldn't be. Those pictures are trying to sell you something. And what sells anything? Sex appeal. Not blatant sex appeal, but what could be called playful sex appeal. In other words: flirting.

So don't overlook the gold mine of flirting techniques that advertising can teach us. Study some ads which feature women and men either singly or together selling products that are for general consumption. Forget the sexually provocative magazines; that's not flirting at all. Focus on the ads which imply that a product or service will spice up your social life.

These ads are the ones that have been tested and shown to work best. Clients and advertisers are convinced that these images "pull." Watch and see which ads and ad campaigns run month after month. If you see the same picture time and time again, you know it draws. And if a smile or gesture, a stance, a look, an apparent glint in the eye will sell cigarettes or garden tools or beauty and grooming products, think how effective these proven formulas will be when you copy them. After all, you aren't selling anything, but are just flirting and sharing a part of yourself with someone else.

The women in *Esquire*, the men in *Cosmopolitan*, the women dancing through the commercial for a man's product, the men who are featured in perfume ads on television, these are excellent examples. And the secret is you don't have to look like these people. You simply have to mimic the gestures, poses, and emotionally charged atmospheres that these marketing efforts present. If you study and adopt these images for your own use, you'll be one step ahead of most flirts.

## WHAT TO MIMIC

**1. Mimic clothing styles.** That's right. Lots of research has gone into what the models are wearing. Is she dressed in a diaphanous dress? Is her hair blowing loosely? Then that's certainly a sexy look, an outfit that a consensus of men would find attractive. So if you are entering a party, a singles bar, or a political rally dressed in that way, and the dress is appropriate to the season, you should get a positive reaction.

The same for men. Is the male model wearing a safari jacket, nice slacks with a crease? Is his tie neatly askew? Then copy this to the best of your ability. Lots of market research has gone into this outfit; more time and thought than you are probably willing to put into your wardrobe. This is from experts; so take heed.

**2. Mimic the setting.** We can't all afford a New York backdrop, but candlelight, a bottle of wine nestled in a cooler, and an inviting couch—these certainly are attainable.

Is this at the beach? What are they carrying? Or sitting on? Are the man and woman looking at paintings in art galleries? Are they eating breakfast in a neat kitchen? Or are they in an office setting that seems a bit more comfortable and inviting than your office does?

**3. Mimic the colors.** If you are decorating your apartment and you want someone of the opposite sex to be comfortable there, look at the settings in which ad agencies put their new products. It will certainly be the newest, most appealing setting. Those high-paid advertising executives feel it has emotional power. And if it has caught your eye in a magazine, they are right.

Colors follow trends, but cool beiges, warm browns, and rich blues all seem to have long-lasting appeal. Remember you are not trying for the cover of *Architectural Digest*; you want love, not pretension.

*For women:* Stay away from women's magazines that may show you the ultimate bedroom: Flowers and lace may make a man think of you as a fourteen year old. Instead, look at the men's magazines to discover their fantasy settings. You don't want to totally neglect your own tastes, but you probably have enough hand-me-downs and personal knickknacks to soften your apartment and give it a feminine look regardless.

*For men:* Forget the men's magazines and the women's magazines. Both of these are too macho or too feminine. Department stores usually present the most neutral and appealing settings for potential flirts. In fact, leaving room for a few vases or accessories gives a woman something to contribute to your apartment. But do have good light in your bathroom. There's nothing more frustrating to a woman checking her makeup than to look good in the bathroom light, and later, glance in your big hall mirror to discover that she has misjudged and made herself up to look like Betty Boop.

**4. Mimic physical gestures.** The exact moment shown in an ad is the ultimate moment of desirability. That's an image you should memorize, for by introducing it into your body language vocabulary, you'll dramatically increase your attractiveness. Is the woman brushing his hand with her jacket, her fingers, her hair? Is the man reaching out to protect, cuddle, or hold the woman? Has his arm not yet reached her shoulder? This is a safe pose.  It shows that the man is close, but not overly assertive.

You might also look at the motion-picture stills that are used to publicize movies. Is there a look in the eye of the male star? Is the actress giving the man a come-hither glance over her shoulder? These are vivid images. This montage, illustration, or photo is the epitome of what market researchers, top advertising agencies, and movie people feel will quickly convey a strong emotion—strong enough to lure customers into the theatres.

You may not have the confidence to do this, but if it's any comfort, you might like to know that some actors and models might feel very silly striking these poses in real life too. They may actually be quite gangly, stilted, and lazy. That's why there are professional writers and directors to make sure that these marvelous-looking people bring just the right attitude to this moment. So be your own writer and director; or, just as good, use the expertise of these people by copying what they think is alluring. Like them, you'll soon achieve the desired effect.

5. **Mimic the mood.** The mood is most important of all. Notice how there is an unhurried feeling to these pictures. On television there is music to enhance the mood. Again you can use tried-and-true techniques, such as playing movie themes. Let these waft through the background. Duplicate the slow, easy, unhurried pace. And take note of how the two people in the ad are somehow in their own, special time capsule. The limited time they have in this special atmosphere becomes very precious. Within it, they create their own reality, free of all distractions.

This is a very important element of successful flirting. If you can create this illusion when flirting, you almost needn't do anything else.

# ♡ 16 ♡
# *The 10 Commandments of Flirting*

**I. THOU SHALT SMILE**

A smile does two things: It warms someone else, and it warms you. So smile, even if you don't feel like it. But don't smile continuously. Give that special person the benefit of your sudden grin. Smiles needn't be bold, either; they can be small, private, conspiratorial, even shy. If you want to smile but are afraid of appearing too forward, you can immediately cover your mouth in some way. Use your hand, a finger; adjust your hair, glasses; touch your chin. These activities soften the body language of your smile, and work for both men and women.

**II. THOU SHALT SHOW GENEROSITY**

Though this may be walking a tightrope, a tiny gift, offering, or trinket given to someone you're flirting with can be as warmly received as a gift from Santa on Christmas Eve. No matter how successful, wealthy, or admired someone is, they never get enough little surprises and gifts. Especially ones that show thought.

A gift can be something to eat, a magazine, a clipped article from the paper, a funny button, a new gadget or household item, something inexpensive that strikes you funny, or something relating to a hobby or interest of your prospective flirting partner. However, this must be small, and you really must not have a lot to lose or gain from giving it. Assume that the person will take it and vanish. If you still want to do this favor, you have the right flirtatious attitude. It must be playful generosity. Then the tiny present will not look like a bribe. The difference between a well-intentioned gift and a bribe lies in your attitude. This technique works for you only if you can give something and forget it. If you are the kind of person who seethes inwardly for years because when your niece was five years old she didn't write you a thank-you note for a five-dollar doll, this gambit is not for you.

## III. THOU SHALT APPROACH FLIRTING PARTNERS AS THOU WOULD A FRIEND

Great flirts extend themselves to *all* the people they like—no matter what their sex is—potential flirting partner or not. Their flirtatious behavior isn't so much flirtatious as it is friendly. (Obvious flirtatious behavior that would only be right for the opposite sex is far too unpolished for flirting experts. By depicting flirts as overly bold, movies and television have done everyone a disservice. Actually this flagrant behavior is a sexual come-on, not a flirtation.)

Here's the secret: ask a new acquaintance, whether male or female, the same questions, offer the same courtesy, and *the same disinterest*.

Do you really care if your best friend doesn't call you after you see a movie together? No. You're confident in the friendship. Well, it is that same tone and demeanor that is most effective when flirting. This gives you a double benefit—you get the warmth that friendship offers, *and* you don't give or get any pressure to move beyond this stage. Of course, most people want to continue a relationship through friendship into dating when they find someone they like. Someone of the opposite sex certainly will respond this way, since you both have even more to gain than friendship—a romance could develop.

How would you approach a friend or new acquaintance? You surely don't think this is the only chance you'll get to initiate a friendship. Though you may zero in on that person, you would still nip the discussion in the bud if you had to go, if you got another phone call, if the person seemed unhappy or not ready to talk, or if you got bored. In friendship, you don't blame yourself if your neighbor isn't in the mood to talk to you because she has to do her laundry . . . but should that neighbor be a man then, oh my goodness, you wonder why you're not worth the time that his sheets are now getting.

To keep on track, convince yourself that this is someone

you'd like to know as a friend, and that is *all* you're going allow yourself to get out of this initial encounter. Someone ι talk to. If you play it right . . . and you exchange telephone numbers (women: absolutely ask for his number too, or else your relationship gets off on an unequal—which can be interpreted as romantic—footing) . . . and this man or woman *is* really a friend . . . then, you can get away with calling, without the onus of asking her for a date or hoping he'll ask you.

### IV. THOU SHALT NURTURE

No one ever gets enough of feeling pampered or being cared for. Do you? So, go over to that woman who's wearing a sweater, and ask if she is cold. Talk to the man guarding his briefcase with his life. Does it contain life-and-death papers? Show concern. Give suggestions. Nurture the things in others that they themselves are nurturing. If a woman dials a telephone with a pencil, is she saving her nails? When a man keeps looking at his watch, does he have to get up early next morning? If the cry of modern society is, "No one really cares about me!" by reversing this, if only briefly, you'll be welcomed with open arms.

Good service personnel do this naturally. Waitresses, stewards, and nurses do this. So does your secretary, your doctor, your broker. Think how overjoyed someone would be to find this nurturing atmosphere in a social setting. Flirts who do this are much sought after—and usually get nurtured themselves.

### V. THOU SHALT SHOW CONCERN FOR A THIRD PERSON OR IDEA

This is most effective when there is an overabundance of flirting going on. That should never stop you, but should cause you to redraw your game plan. If others are being flirtatious, you can be too. But for most people, an atmosphere of aggressive sexuality makes it necessary to fall back on this plan.

First, assume that your potential flirting partner is delighted with the attention, but also a bit embarrassed.

Secondly, approach him as you would a brother or a sister. You want advice, not warmth, not a drink, not pity. And you approach him while you are exerting your personal power in the direction of another potential flirting partner.

You might be bold and say that you wonder if he knows that man across the room, you'd like to meet him. If anything but a "Yup" escapes from the mouth of the man you are with, you have begun a conversation. And if he asks, "Why that person?" or makes any other small talk, you simply act toward this other man in the way you'd like to act with the man you're with.

Or suppose a man is dying to talk with a lovely woman. If he exerts his personal power 100 percent in her direction, he'll come on far too strong. Yet, if he confides to this new woman that his ex-girl friend just came in and he doesn't know how to handle this, there's a good bet this companion will sprout lots of advice on how to deal with a former love.

Celebrities have a very common ploy that works on the same principle. Since you obviously know who they are, they don't have to impress you with how powerful, terrific, or lovely they are. *People* magazine has handled that chore for them. So, they are able to win over new loves and friends simply by confiding their problems. Their problems become the third interest that you both focus on.

Now, for all of us non-celebrities, confiding very personal problems to a stranger is probably unwise. But confiding rather common difficulties without getting into the specifics, again acts as that "third interest."

Causes, complaints, and weather conditions are other third-party substitutes. You can hate the smog, the baby-seal killers, and the devalued franc, all the while stirring up those passions within you for the person at your side. And a confluence of these things is even better. Should the man that you both favor for president make a foolish remark, the weather get so bad your flirting partner can't enjoy a favorite sport, and the superintendent turn down the heat at work, you and your flirting partner are in the perfect climate for advanced flirting. That's why rain, heat, snow, and disaster produce not only good strong mail couriers, but some of the most romantic evenings imaginable.

## VI. THOU SHALT CENSOR THY THOUGHTS AND ACTIONS

Censoring doesn't mean you should worry or fret about the impression you are making, but it does mean you should *think* before you act. Think before you do or say anything that might rock the boat. Don't assume that you are talking with your mother or your secretary or your business manager. Your quirks may be endearing to them, since they know some of the nicer things about you. But don't spring negatives on someone new who doesn't have the benefit of knowing the more conventional side of your personality.

Less is really more, even when flirting. Should you wear your loud, red plaid jacket? Should you be the most overdressed or underdressed woman at a party? For beginning flirts, you probably should not. Of course, you'll want to stand out, but not because of something that can be construed as lack of taste or style.

And while we are on taste, four-letter words are a no-no. Some people are disturbed by them, and unless your vocabulary is severely limited, you'll come out ahead by dropping these words.

Along with censoring what you wear, say, and do, censor yourself as to what you will put up with. Is someone treating you badly? Get away, even if she is the first woman vice-president of your bank. Don't let your passions for flirting allow you to subject yourself to negative people, talk, or actions.

Flirting must be done in a safe emotional environment, which is why you must censor yourself and your atmosphere before you flirt. Then, and only then, will you be comfortable enough to relax and be magnificent.

## VII. THOU SHALT ALWAYS KEEP SOMETHING IN RESERVE

One of the problems flirts face is that they are so generous that when they can't give, they feel inadequate. And they sometimes give away too much. No matter how much you want to impress someone with your sensuality, your wit, your specialness, your attractiveness, and your unique style, don't go overboard at the beginning of a flirtatious cycle and reveal all your wondrous achievements at once. Keep something in reserve.

Why? Why not use every asset you have to attract a new flirting partner? Because if you used every asset, he or she would be so intimidated and bowled over that they'd back away. Sure, you might be Wonder Woman or Superman, but you're not the person they want to buy a beer for.

Keeping something in reserve when you flirt gives two concomitant messages. It tells your partner subliminally that you aren't going "all out" for him. This, in turn, makes you more mysterious, more approachable, and more vulnerable.

Holding something in reserve does not mean keeping news of your wife or husband under wraps. It is not lying by omission. It is doling out information about yourself piecemeal, so others can savor every detail. After all, you are simply flirting, and you want to save something for the man or woman you decide to make a more substantial commitment to.

Treat your flirting life as you treat chocolate. You love it, you savor it, but you don't gobble it up all at once. What? You do! Then follow the ritual of chocaholics. Keep something in reserve (a Snickers, some chocolate-chip ice cream, some Mounds); that way, whether with chocolate or with flirting, you'll never have to venture out in the cold to satisfy your cravings.

## VIII. THOU SHALT REMEMBER THE POWER OF TOUCH

Flirts do something that no other people do, except lovers. Flirts not only display their emotional warmth through their attention and interest, they also fulfill the need we all have to be touched.

Naturally, how you touch someone is very, very important. When you are flirting, never touch someone anywhere where there might be direct sexual overtones. Because the most flirtatious touching is a touch that I call "parental." A parental touch is one of assurance, warmth, and protection. And when you are flirting, what you really want to convey with touch is not a sexual message, but a caring message.

So how do you touch a flirting partner? Very, very lightly. You never grab or push or bump someone. (So tacky!) You stroke someone lightly, you squeeze, and you brush. Brushing is really the best early flirting technique. A woman can brush lint off a man's jacket. He can brush the hair out of her eyes.

Another method is finger walking. Remember those telephone ads, "Let your fingers do the walking through the Yellow Pages? "And you see two fingers walking up a telephone book? Used for a couple of seconds, this technique is half message, half child's play, and totally flirtatious.

Too shy to try these? Then you can touch someone's hand with your hand as you make a point. Your touching gesture can actually help you punctuate a sentence. A touch can mean any of the following: "Listen," Wow," "Okay," "But wait," "Really?" "Now?" "What time is it?" "Someone's listening to our conversation," "I agree," and lots more.

To make this little touch work in perfect syncopation with your words, you must finish half a phrase, take a little beat, breathe, touch your flirting partner, and before you have finished the two-second (*only* two seconds) touch, start saying the words which complete your thought.

To simplify: You stop in the middle of a sentence, wait half a second, breathe in, breathe out and simultaneously touch your partner, hold the touch for a count of two, and as you raise your hand finish your sentence.

And finally there's the accidental touch. You both reach for the saltshaker at the same time, or the typewriter ribbon; or you both try to catch a falling dish. This kind of touch—the unexpected—is probably the best of all. And how can you tell it was of the electrifying, flirtatious variety? Because after touching one another, you'll each imperceptibly brush off the part of the hand that touched. As if to prove that (a) it was accidental, and (b) you are checking for damage. Why? Because (c) the romantic sparks were undeniable.

### IX. THOU SHALT MAKE MISTAKES

The more mistakes you make early on in your flirting career, the faster you are going to become a fabulous flirt. You need to be adventurous and try things. And to really fail, to realize that your come-hither stare distorts your face into a Halloween mask, may not be pleasant, but is definitely helpful.

All of the successful flirts I know said they started out making loads of mistakes—and I certainly made my share. Both my men and women friends said they started to learn about flirting because they felt they were so incompetent. They decided they had nothing to lose by making really bad mistakes, and so consciously didn't worry about doing that at first.

One man described his "Johnny Carson technique." He explained that, as an admirer of Johnny, he noticed that Johnny got his biggest laughs from the way he handled a joke that *didn't* go over with the audience. Some say Johnny's ready answers for these flubs are as arduously prepared by his writers as the regular jokes. So this outrageously flirtatious man figured that he'd do the same thing. He assumed that his lines or gestures would be rejected by women. (He later told me that some of his boldest moves were most successful, claiming that you can't figure women.) And he had memorized a series of comebacks for each situation, so that as the women laughed with him, he was able to reveal his soft interior.

This man is now so smooth, that it appears he moves on wheels, but he still tries to make mistakes.

"They make me seem less manipulative and controlling. And women become less fearful immediately."

So consider mistakes as much a part of your flirting repertoire as anything else. And have a few ready comebacks. They ought not to be flip remarks or put-downs—either to yourself or your flirting partner. Just phrases that show a man or woman that you may have been overly assertive, and now you realize "your mistake."

### X. THOU SHALT MAKE MEMORIES

Flirting makes memories. And the best flirts make the best memories with and for their flirting partners, because their flirting makes the other person feel so good. Memories, too, can be enhanced—and not just with Barbra Streisand singing in the background.

Memories do two things: Firstly, they make you and the other people remember an occasion and one another. Secondly, they provide social glue that keeps you a part of a society or a club or a clique. If you are remembered as the man who put up the decorations for the Sadie Hawkins Day dance, who's going to remember that you didn't appear at one club meeting all year long? You were there for the memories. That's what counts. Memorable occasions and the people who attend them stick in everyone's mind.

Memories add to a feeling of camaraderie. If you tell a woman, "I saw you at the boat race last summer," this dispels many of her suspicions about you, because you have a record of being in a certain group.

Memories are built upon three separate tiers of experience.

**Stage 1—Discussion and anticipation.** This can be talking about your vacation, for example; planning it, figuring out how to pay for it. All this adds to the vacation's importance and will give you a larger emotional payoff from this adventure.

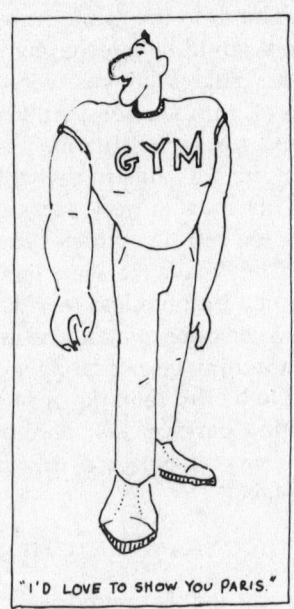

"I'D LOVE TO SHOW YOU PARIS."

In flirting, start talking about the next time you might see your flirting partner. Build up the expectation. Or plan on doing something with this person that is special. Men often say something like, I'd love to show you Paris, or Mexico, or my hometown. No matter how flippantly this is said, the woman will remember. You have created—depending upon how much more you mention this —a potentially powerful memory.

**Stage 2—The memory itself.** Most special days are fraught with worry and anxiety; the real thing is not as good as the memory. Rome was fun and enjoyable, but do you remember how cold it was last May? No. You remember that fabulous dinner overlooking the Coliseum. Why? Because you had talked and planned and looked forward to seeing that monument your entire life. You did not look forward to, or dwell on, the cold weather.

Punch up the memory while you are making it; get some souvenirs. Keep a hat from a party. Take a picture. Buy a postcard or knickknack. Or bring something home, or have something framed. (Think of this as pre-garage sale purchasing.) Encapsulate any part of the memory you can. No matter how corny this may seem, your partner in this memory will get caught up in your delight. It's hard not to, as it is so flattering to him or her when you remember, fondly, the time you spent together.

**Stage 3—Discuss these memories every chance you get.** "I remember how beautiful you looked at that Labor Day dance." "What a great time we had camping; remember how clear the sky was? You surely can't see one-tenth of those stars tonight."

Memories don't have to be monumental social occasions. They can be, "Last night you were really funny. You were wittier than anyone else there." Or, "I can still remember how you told that bartender off; boy, was he scared." Or, "When you got in that debate over taxes with that lawyer, you made him look so silly, I'll bet he'll never get in an argument with you again."

When you reminisce about these incidents, weaving new ones in with the old, you are forging emotional bonds that are hard to break. That's how great flirts make the most of even the most minimal flirting encounter.

# ♡ 17 ♡
# *How to Create a Flirtatious First Impression*

SINCE MOST FLIRTING NEVER GETS PAST THE STAGE OF FIRST IMPRESSIONS, THESE FIRST GLIMPSES ARE CRUCIAL IN DECIDING IF A FLIRTATION WILL CONTINUE OR WILL END. (Of course, you as an expert flirt will look beyond first impressions to the real person inside. But you can't expect your partners to be so thoughtful.)

Here's how to make the first impression you give count.

## YOUR IMAGE

There are two things that can change a person's image overnight—clothes and winning a lottery. Until you do the latter, here are the flirting clothes that should be in your wardrobe.

**For Men:** Navy blue blazer with gold buttons; gray slacks to go with this. (An essential for any man over the age of twelve.)

A tweed jacket with patches on the elbows. (For some reason women either really love this look or don't notice it, so you can't go wrong. A very good "intellectual" look.)

Khaki slacks to go with long- or short-sleeved shirts.

Your shoes should always be loafers. But forget the tassels unless you are still in college. (Loafers make you appear more casual and easygoing. Save the wing tips for the wedding.)

A further suggestion. For important occasions, check the length of your slacks, and shorten or lengthen them, if necessary. Women notice this—a lot!

All of the above project sincerity, will not seem overly authoritative, and will give you an "approachable" air when flirting with women. You need to have a look that works with your subtle approach to flirting. Stay away from gold chains (if a woman thinks you should wear one, you'll get one on your next birthday), dark suits and vests (unless you live in

Washington, D.C., or are going after a woman with an MBA), and safari outfits (at best she'll assume you've already been on that trip to Africa without her. At worst she'll think you are a man searching for a hobby).

**For Women:** A black cocktail dress that you can relax in without worrying that you appear overweight.

A navy skirt that will go well with any type of blouse. (Navy is the next best thing to virginal white in a woman's wardrobe.)

A red dress. (This isn't necessarily great for flirting. Too overpowering. But you need one for those times when you know you'll see an ex at a party and you want to be the center of attention.)

Any pair of shorts, short skirt, or culottes that look good with an alligator shirt. Yes, alligators are out, but since it takes most men about two years to figure out what's in and what isn't, you'll be right in step.

One preppy outfit. (When it works, a man will bring you home to meet the family trust fund. If it doesn't work he won't notice you anyway, so you get another shot at flirting with him, next time, when you change your outfit.)

One pair of high heels. (You don't have to be able to walk in them for long, but it's nice if you can get them back on your feet after taking them off during dinner or a movie.)

A slit skirt. (Yes, it must go all the way up.)

A little business suit that fits like a dream, one on which the first button keeps popping open. (Don't wear this for business, but for flirting it projects a wonderfully competent, while slightly vulnerable image.)

A pair of shoes you can walk in. (They must look good, feel good, and you must be able to keep them on your feet for those long walks in the rain.)

High boots. (Only for the flirting adventurers. Definitely effective for men who like women with a bit of verve. However, you'll have to combine them with other garments that show vulnerability, or the man could think you are overly forward.)

A wonderful angora sweater the color of your eyes, your skin, or your hair. (There are multiple benefits here. First, the color; secondly, the texture; thirdly, the bits of lint left behind by the angora—something to remind him of you when he's dressing the next day.)

Textured stockings. (Men either love them or not. But try—boldly. With legs you can afford to be overtly sexy.)

A swimsuit you look good in. (And as extra protection, put it on every day of your life to make sure you can get into this creation when you get a special invitation. Swimsuits that models and starlets wear are too bold. You want to project much more class than that, so pick a rather conservative style. Let your body do the work, not the suit.)

A good-looking coat. (One that doesn't make you look fifty pounds heavier than you already are. I'd say "slimming" but that is asking for too much. Yes, fur is always flirtatious; men love it. So forget that it makes you look like a giant panda.)

## Color

**For Women:** Navy blue, white, black, and light blue are favorites of men. However, men always notice a woman in a red dress or hot pink outfit. Forget gray, wine, olive green, and chocolate brown; they remind men of the army.

**For Men:** Women like light colors. For shirts, pale blue, yellow, blue and white stripes, and beige. For business suits, stay with the sincerity of navy; pin-striped only if you're in the East. As a second choice, gray is good—it's non-threatening but a little lacking in pizzazz. For sporting outfits, stick with blue and dark green. If your sports wardrobe could be mistaken for the flag of any country, wave this outfit good-bye. Although brown and black are nice colors, too much of them can be a real turn-off. Plaids are okay as long as they aren't big enough to play tick-tack-toe on.

## Accessories

Women have it a bit easier than men. There is no way a brief-case can be flirtatious just standing there. But a woman's purse was invented to flirt with. And it's got to be a purse, not a satchel. Satchels are for lugging your stuff over to a man's apartment, after you've met him. Purses are for meeting a man in the first place. Which are best? Small purses. As one man said, "I don't want to feel like I've got to wonder what's in that thing?"

Shoulder bags are flirtatious, because women can whip them around, fling them on and off their shoulders, and generally get a lot of play out of them. However, they can look like seat belts if they aren't really sized to your frame. And men don't want to feel you are strapped in. Get one sized for you.

Sorry, but shoulder bags for men are out, unless it is definitely a piece of luggage.

Hand purses are trouble. They look nice but a man doesn't want to reach for your hand only to discover that it's taken up with a clutch purse. Get these only if you have given up flirting.

Scarves can be used like purses, but are even more flirty. You can adjust a scarf, take it off, wrap your hair in it, all things that get you to stretch and flaunt your body in such an unobvious way. Again the drawback. Most men think scarves detract from your looks. (Thick winter scarves are exceptions. Men like these because it makes them feel that they could play in the snow with you.) And scarves do provide a psychological barrier. This may be fine at work, but while flirting, it makes you seem a bit too unavailable.

What can a man do? The classic cliché: Loosen your tie and unbutton your collar. That is a very flirtatious thing to do. Still, many women think that men who wear ties loosened (unless they were planned to be worn loose) appear sloppy. Also men who loosen their ties, and take them off in the middle of a date seem somewhat gross to women. ("I think he must have a problem getting dressed up. Can't he keep his clothes on a minute longer?") There are exceptions. For instance, if you are stuck in an elevator with others. After eight or nine hours waiting to be rescued, you can undo your tie, but should fix it as soon as the elevator is working again. If you undo your tie, take it off, and take your jacket off as well. Undoing a tie should mark informality, not that you can no longer endure the neckline pressure.

## Jewelry

Much to my dismay, it seems to be a turn-off for both men and women. Men say that jewelry makes a woman look older (honestly, they say this), cheaper (even if it's *real*), more available, and less nice than a woman who wears little or no jewelry.

And earrings? They think it's best to be without. Pierced

earrings terrify them. (What if I rip her ear off when we're kissing?) Men especially hate earrings that could double as hubcaps.

Women like men without wedding rings best of all. But they like the men with wedding rings better than the married men without them. Pinky rings and chains are out, but nice watches are sexy. Women prefer the old-fashioned, non-digital watches on a man. (Those usually show a man with sensitivity.)

## YOUR PERSONAL GROOMING

**For Men:** Good grooming means naturalness: Hair and clothes that are not overly styled, muscles that are not overly intimidating. Women like hair that moves. Especially when it has been moved into that shape by a man-made blow-dryer. No blow-drying isn't natural, but somehow the slick, soft, sculptured look it gives a man's hair makes a woman want to touch it, and him. Hair that seems overly cared for, and this applies to beards and mustaches, in some ways makes a man seem less, not more masculine. However, successful women flirts say that a man with a mustache, beard, or overly styled hair is easier to approach, because he seems so in need of personal compliments.

Fitness isn't much of a turn-on for women. Flirtatious women say that a man's perfect physique or blatantly overmuscled body gives out strong but intimidating signals. This perfection makes a woman think twice before approaching him. However, if he approaches her and is interested in talking about things of a casual nature, his fitness appears to be a plus.

Flirtatious women also like men to wear a fragrance, because this shows the man cares, which makes him seem more approachable. Women dislike, however, the flagrant use of those breath-sprays. "So gauche. Men use them even three feet from your own face. It's like he's saying, sure she'll kiss me, and to prove what a sweet guy I am, I'm going to spruce myself up." Male flirts say that breath mints are very successful with women. As for toothpicks, flicking a Bic on and off, or playing with a straw—forget it—these things denote nervousness to women.

What helps a man flirt successfully? A nice clean look. Over-grooming, primping, and constant smoothing-out of clothes makes a woman feel that the man is too self-absorbed. Though these may just be signs of nervousness, they nevertheless project something else. Successful male flirts have other ways to dispel nervousness. They sit back and watch the world go on around them. They don't pace or talk or fiddle with anything. As a non-smoker said, "These are the times that cigarettes were invented for." But successful male flirts say that cigarette smoking, though the perfect "thing" to do at this nervous time, usually puts up an invisible barrier between them and women. Women are less likely to engage in conversation with a man sitting by himself if he is smoking. The flirt who can sit still and do nothing—neither drink, smoke, nor fidget—is most likely to find a woman cozying up to him.

**For Women:** Hair is one of the great flirting props. Playing with hair, not combing it, but pushing it, shaking it, and twisting it are very sexy come-ons. Successful women flirts say that playing with their hair is the single most seductive, but non-threatening, gesture they give to men.

As for nails. Either men want them long and painted deep red, or they don't care at all. Still women with medium-length nails, lightly colored, seem to please every category of male perfectionist.

Fragrance is another matter. Many men say they can remember the fragrance a woman whom they loved used. Yet just about all of them say that they dislike perfume. And that if they don't like the scent a woman is wearing, she is automatically disqualified as a flirting partner. So, it's safest to wear nothing. Which, oddly enough, is more appealing to men than anything. And if you do wear a fragrance, put on half of whatever you normally put on. Men complain that women often overdose on perfume, even if it's a fragrance they like.

Fitness is an absolute plus for women flirts. Men not only like women who work out (men like narcissistic women, yet women do not like narcissistic men), but successful women flirts project an energy, a life, a feeling of activity and grace. Even if a man is not interested in physical fitness himself, he likes the fact that the woman in his life is. And physical beauty is not the ultimate for men. Many flirtatious men don't differentiate between someone who has a great body and someone who is downright pretty. Still women who have beautiful faces as well as good bodies, do have an edge over others. But men, thank goodness, realize that these luminous creatures are few and far between.

Very often, male flirts say that women who are average looking but fit, appear most vulnerable and interesting to them. What matters most to them are a nice figure and nice hair, which shows that beauty is within reach of most women who make an effort.

As for makeup, women should chuck most of it. The things that seem indispensable—blusher, eyeliner, and lipstick—are the very things men say women overdo. Too much blush makes for an overly made-up, and, thus, an older and sometimes cheaper look. As for eyeliner and eyeshadow, not one man I know has said that he thought these added to a woman. Mascara is another matter. Men like it a lot. But they feel that lipstick is overdone, and the deeper, darker colors are just the opposite of kissable. Natural lipstick is most attractive. And men like the smooth, one-color look that foundation gives when lightly applied. Male flirts say it makes a woman look more put together and "naturally" pretty.

## FLIRTATIOUS BODY TALK

While you are saying all the right things to put a prospective flirting partner in the mood, your body is playing a melody underneath your words. And it better not be Saturday Night Fever. It is essential that your words and deeds match. If your body is not in harmony with what you are saying you can expect your flirting maneuvers to be successful with only the most superficial people. (And you don't need a book on flirting for that; all you need is a reservation at a singles bar.) But good, honest flirting takes the coordination of a trapeze artist, because all your physical responses—not just your gestures—must be in synch for your words to be effective.

We all have a built-in nonsense detector, a sixth sense, a psychic ability for testing whether someone is being honest. And when we know something is wrong, there is no way in the world we can think of a person as sexy, attractive, or interesting.

The judicious use of our bodies is what can turn a minor

encounter into a grand amour. Just think of all the couples who have fallen in love with one another when they didn't even speak the same language.

## Eyes

Your eyes help you discriminate between those you'd like to flirt with and those you'll pass on. But they also can ignite or extinguish the flames of flirting possibilities. While staring or holding a gaze a second longer than usual will succeed in attracting notice, so will other subtle and more tasteful eye contact. Try this: Throw a glance to a person, and then, as soon as your flirting partner turns to meet your gaze, immediately lower your eyes. This is every effective for both men and women.

Another technique that successful male flirts use is the darting eye. Women have less luck with this because it is a bit aggressive and somehow has masculine connotations. Take a quick look at a woman once; then return your eyes to their normal position; take a second look, held much longer; and then a third look where you turn your head in her direction but do not direct your eyes at her. The third move makes you appear less intrusive, but still confronts her in a manageable way.

A technique that works for men and women, the sensual, bedroom-eyes look, can be achieved this way. Simply hold back blinking. Your eyes will get wider and wider. The trick is *not* to raise your forehead in any way; let your eyes and eyelids do all the work. Do not lower the lids to give what you think is a veiled sexy look—this only looks ridiculous. After not blinking for as long as you can, blink. As you blink, hold your eyes closed a smidgen longer than you'd normally do. Not blinking may cause your eyes to tear a little, which makes them look soft and limpid, and bound to melt someone's heart.

Blinking, rubbing your eyes, even checking your eye makeup surreptitiously, can also affect a flirting partner (contact-lens wearers have known this for quite a while) as a seeming reversal of the flirtatious stare. Someone seeing those actions would interpret them as a reluctance to flirt in a more direct manner, which is a plus. You also appear vulnerable, approachable, and in a mood to flirt. And you have so carefully masked your intentions, that if a prospective flirting partner doesn't respond, or if you are flirting with someone who is already with another partner, you can never be accused of flirting.

## Hands

Your hands, though a subtler flirting indicator and signal, are still very effective, even from a distance. Successful flirts try not to fidget, but if they do, they at least fidget in a manner that has some rhythm to it. Rhythmic repetitions are very soothing and alluring. So when you rub your keys or play with a prop, do it not in a jerking or bold manner, but with controlled, rhythmic repetitions.

The most flirtatious part of the hand is the wrist. The inner wrist. So, any movements where you inadvertently reveal the inner wrist to your flirting partner can be disarming. Maybe this is the reason that wristwatches play such a role in flirting manners. Looking at a wristwatch necessitates turning your inner wrist towards another person, and outrageous flirts do this with exaggerated movements. Another use of the inner wrist is in the yawning stretch—cross your hands in front of you, turning both wrists toward the other person.

Hands and arms using certain clear signals can put off a prospective flirt and mark you as unapproachable. Among these negative flirting signals are any movements in which you cross your arms or hands in front of you. Crossing arms or hands to the side implies dual meanings. (Use only when you want to be truly ambiguous.) It is almost as if you are sending the message, "Don't come to me, but if you do, do it in a circuitious way."

Follow these rules about using your arms and hands to flirt. If you can somehow form a circle with your arms and hands, you are creating a very open, positive, inviting body position. However, whenever you are crossed (even in an inexact manner) you are excluding potential flirting encounters. In flirting, think openness. So open hand movements are good. Closed fists are negative. An open, outstretched palm is good. Palms down, on a table or in your lap, are anti-flirtatious. And hands resting not up or down but on edge, are giving an uncertain flirting signal, probably very good in coordination with other flirting actions. Hands should either tone down or accompany your other flirting maneuvers.

## Legs

Crossed legs or ankles can be flirtatious on women, if not done in a clenched manner. Men should stick with crossed ankles. However, both men and women should cross their legs in the direction of the person they are flirting or trying to flirt with. Undoing and crossing your legs or ankles in this position, sitting with your legs uncrossed in-between, carries an excellent flirting message and a very sexual one.

## FLIRTATIOUS PROPS

You can never lose when using flirtatious props, because they give you a perfect flirting excuse. What! Someone doesn't appreciate your forward comments? Well, it's not your fault. You were just trying to find out if they were flying on a supersaver ticket when you were paying full fare. Or trying to get your grocery cart in line. Or you're sorry, but you thought the newspaper left behind belonged to them. Whoops!

### The Umbrella

An umbrella doesn't have to be open to be a seductive prop. In fact, you don't even need the rain. First, you can always forget it, forcing you to return to where you left it, giving a flirting partner another chance to get your phone number. When your umbrella doesn't open, your hands and your flirting partner's hands can innocently (!) touch as you struggle to reattach the fabric to those bent wires. Since umbrellas are always slipping, falling, and getting in people's ways (What, you didn't plan to trip that attractive man as he entered the restaurant?), you can apologize. Outdoors with an umbrella, you can touch or get closer because the rain is still getting you wet. Incidentally, the rain is a great flirting prop, but unreliable. Being wet and uncomfortable gives you and a fellow flirting partner something to complain about together.

### The Sunglasses

Another universal flirting prop. The way people buy these things, you'd think everyone was living at the equator. How sunny is it anyway? But why think realistically? Natural flirts know that the covering and uncovering of the eyes is magical. First there is nothing, then something, then nothing. It's a virtual striptease of the eyes. Then there's pushing the sunglasses over your head. Adjusting the glasses, rubbing your eyes. All these gestures are totally flirtatious. Even if you  never wear glasses, get sunglasses to play with. You'll be delighted with the response.

## The Mirror

This is a flirting privilege denied men. Using a mirror, gazing into it, or discreetly touching up makeup (but not really putting it on), are all appealing flirtatious actions to a man. Here's how it works. Sit sideways anywhere from ten to fifty feet away from a man. Take out your mirror and place it between you and the man (in direct line with him). Then smooth your mascara or eyeshadow back into place. It is even permissible to add a bit of lip gloss and play with your lips. There is something very seductive about applying gloss with your finger, but putting on lipstick from a tube is déclassé.

## The Car

Your car can be a flirtatious vehicle or just transportation, depending on how you groom it. Flash isn't important, but order is. First, forget having anything hanging at the mirror. And bumper stickers ought to be non-suggestive and rather new. Get them off your bumper when they're torn or faded. Little cars seem most approachable and fun to others. One successful flirt actually moved down to a less expensive, smaller car, because she felt her big car put off men. Using your back seat as a garbage dump is not appealing. Neither is having your dry cleaning clumped in the back seat—that's what your trunk is for. However, one nice touch is having tissues in the car—always a sign of someone eminently vulnerable. Handiwipes are not. Apparently it's more desirable to cry in your car than to eat junk food.

*Special tip*: Want to meet a man you see on the freeway each morning? Put a sign with your phone number on it in your back window—announcing your car is for sale. To be sure of a response, list a ridiculously low figure.

## Home Crafts

The "I made it myself" secret flirting gesture. Remember how mom was always thrilled when you drew a picture of a horse, even though everyone else thought it looked like a pig? Well, home crafts bring out that same response in caring flirting partners. (And if they don't have compassion, you might as well know it right away.) Making food or crafts (drawing, sculpting, building, or designing something), and then sharing it with someone does make a flirt vulnerable. You mustn't expect everyone to feel the instant intimacy, but many times this will work like a dream, and will immediately allow you to talk about less superficial things than you might have before.

## Flowers

Men will do better with one, two, or three buds, than with the whole rose garden. Big bouquets put women on the spot. (Women assume that a bouquet, at the beginning of a relationship, pressures them. However, only a heel wouldn't send a dozen of her favorite flowers after an important relationship milestone.) And forget those artificaly colored blossoms you get at freeway off-ramps. Who are you kidding? Everyone knows they were a last-minute thought, and a cheap one at that. Better to buy one flower. If you can't resist getting the bouquets, put most of the blooms away and give your flirting companion only one flower anyway. Besides, when that bud dies, you can say, "What a shame," and bring a new flower!

The same doesn't hold true for women giving men flowers. Maybe men just can't appreciate the beauty of roses, or their macho pride won't let them. But I found that even a single thornless rose made a man uncomfortable and pressured—and believe it or not, he thought less, not more, of the woman. Better to save the bud for your favorite girl friend.

## Aspirin

Flirts know how to turn a disadvantage into an asset. Take, for instance, the proverbial bedtime headache. Flirts do just the opposite. They get a headache whenever they see someone they're attracted to. The difference is they go up to this person and ask for two aspirin.

This activates anyone's Florence Nightingale spirit. If your partner is even marginally interested, Mr. or Ms. Nightingale will apply a cool, lovely, sexy hand to your forehead. (Just to see how sick you really are, of course!)

Touché! You have done the impossible: You've made the first *emotional* move, but let your flirting partner make the first *physical* one.

# ♡ 18 ♡
# *How to Flirt from Any Position*

IN THE BEGINNING YOU NEED TRICKS, DEVICES TO MAKE FLIRT-ING WORK FOR YOU. Otherwise, you are so wrapped up in a self-conscious feeling that you project nervousness instead of sensuality. But get a few practical gestures under your belt, and you'll soon be a freewheeling flirting sprite. Yes, it is orchestrated. But even orchestras rehearse. So think of yourself as a musician. Practice these fundamentals; afterwards, you can improvise.

## SITTING

Men and women who are flirting would do best to imitate talk show guests. Picture your potential flirting partner as the audience, and think of the telephone, your newspaper, or a pal as Johnny Carson. Talk to Johnny, lean towards Johnny, but play the audience. A trick outrageous flirts use is to draw a circle with their arms so they include their flirting partners in their present activity.

If you are reading a paper, turn the pages so that on every turn one arm or the other has to move not only directly opposite your flirting partner, but past this person. Think of a clock. If you are sitting at twelve o'clock and your flirting partner is at three o'clock, then move through three o'clock all the way to four o'clock when making these sweeping arm gestures.

Reaching down to touch your shoe, purse, or belongings, *without* paying direct attention to these movements, delivers a very important flirting message—that you can do these things without giving them a second thought; so maybe, just maybe, you are that much more interested in your flirting partner. The "I can do many things at one time" message converts into a strong flirtatious gesture, because then every single action takes on more significance.

For men sitting alone, a briefcase is the perfect prop. It can be juggled, set down, locked, and unlocked, all using the sweeping-arm-gesture routine.

Sitting in low plush couches or chairs is unflirtatious, unless you curl up on them. Leaning back and disappearing in a seat puts you in a bad light and makes you seem sluggish. So if you are forced to disappear into plushness, do so with your feet up.

If you want to sit flirtatiously on airplanes, there is no way you can arrive at your destination looking good. But many men and women make the sacrifice. If you must stretch out, get a blanket (they make both men and women look cute and vulnerable); otherwise you look gangly and uncoordinated. Coordination is important in flirting, because while you may want to appear appealing and accessible, uncoordination reeks of being either confused, unconfident, or drunk.

## STANDING

Appearing flirtatious while standing requires a lot of mental energy. Although you want to appear still (you are standing, after all), you don't want to look like a department store dummy, nor do you want to seem jittery and wired up, as if you're taking a break from your flashdancing routine. So the energy has to be in your mind.

If you are standing, you appear most vulnerable, yet at the same time unapproachable. Your height (even if it's only five feet) forms a protective barrier around you. But being all alone —not leaning on a stool or anything—makes you seem accessible. The mental ploy here is to think energy without displaying it. No tapping your toes, no drumming your fingers. If you feel musical, take up an instrument, but don't flirt.

How do you think energy? Think of something exciting. In your mind debate the pros and cons of an issue. Go over your job; decide if it is the right career route for you. Do not dwell on past romantic rejections, the worst parties you've ever attended, who hasn't returned your phone calls or money. Fantasize about a trip, a new hobby, sport, or, best of all, what might transpire while you are waiting. Positive thoughts radiate. Negative thoughts only attract more negative experiences.

Do change positions every two or three minutes, but not every second. If you are at a party, do a mental count of all the people there. Pretend you have to guess how many guests are actively in therapy. All guessing games are good, because you lose your self-consciousness then.

If you are standing, it is always very flirtatious to put your back directly to the person you are most interested in. (Why does she have her back to me, he'll think?) Some of the most outrageous flirts say they have developed a special form of radar. They can tell when they are getting close to a person they want to flirt with. They also have learned the knack of backing closer and closer into the conversational circle of a hoped for flirting partner.

## ENTERING A ROOM

This simple act requires the coordination of a drill team. The proof? All successful flirts have a set routine. Several admitted that they choreographed this maneuver once, and now repeat it religiously. Here's the way to do it.

**Beat 1—Enter room and plant yourself.** Open the door and stop immediately at the entrance of the room.

**Beat 2—Turn around and back.** Take a deep breath and turn around about half a turn. If there is a door, turn as if something has just fallen off the wall behind you, but don't turn all the way around. If there is no door closed behind you, turn about 160 degrees to see what is going on (you heard something, didn't you?). You should move your head and maybe your upper torso, but keep your feet planted firmly in the flirtatious standing position you first assumed when you entered the room. (This is something you'll want to perfect on your own. Many women put their feet at right angles to one another. Men prefer to just have one foot ahead of the other.)

Standing and averting your gaze helps make the people in the room more comfortable. They see you turning, seemingly defenseless, and can check you out without you seeing them.

**Beat 3—Look into the room again.** Only now you look down about one foot lower than most of the people's heads in the room.

**Beat 4—Take a big breath.** This just happens to expand your chest and is considered a blatant flirting sign. But you are not being blatant because you are doing this for an entire room. While breathing in, you must look in a direction about 45 to 90 degrees away from the direction you are soon going to walk. Again, you are letting the people see your profile, which is flirtatious and disarming. And if you have a "best side," like Barbra Streisand, make sure you always look in that direction. (It is up to you to force the people in the room to accommodate this peculiarity.)

**Beat 5—A half-smile.** Practice in a mirror. You don't want to look like a grinning hyena, you want to seem happy, confident, but not giddy. At the same time, walk in the direction of your flirting destination. If you don't know where it is, just go 45 to 90 degrees away from where you were looking in BEAT 4.

You have just made a dynamite entrance. As the male flirt who invented this said, "It is the best kind of flirtatious attention-getting. You are noticed, but not scrutinized, the best possible position for a flirt to be in."

## LEAVING A ROOM

This is a different story. First, never make a big point of saying good-bye to everyone. (They need you to tell them the party's over?) If you can't find the host or hostess in one pass around the room or the party, stop looking, and send flowers the next day. The look of a lost homing pigeon diminishes the positive image you projected throughout the gathering.

On the other hand, never, ever, rush out, not even if your parking meter has run out. And never walk in a straight line; it makes you look like you're leading a fire drill.

# ♡ 19 ♡
# *How to Flirt in Any Situation*

### ORDERING A DRINK

Good flirts know what they want in a drink. However, the rule of "me too" works flirtatiously when ordering beverages, especially alcohol.

Doing the same things as your flirting partner creates harmony. Ordering the same dinner, drink, ice-cream flavor, toothpaste (or at least using what your host has), even using the same discount, long distance telephone service brings camaraderie. ("Remember the night they only had Peach Daiquiri mix at the ski tavern?" or "Hi! Are you sick this morning? Me too. Must have been that Duck L'Orange we had last night.")

So if you can stomach it, or are good at nursing a drink, have what your flirting partner orders. But what if she orders a drink with more fruit in it than on Carmen Miranda's hat? Order a straight, simple, easy drink, but ask to taste hers. What if he orders a double bourbon straight up, and downs it in one gulp? Order a club soda. After that macho exercise, he'll want one too.

### HANDLING INTRODUCTIONS

Always put out your hand. Always say the person's name when grasping the hand. Always ask a question, "How do you know our host?" "What part of Chicago are you from?" "Do you always come here?" "Why you don't look the part, role, position; what a nice surprise!"

Introductions usually just lie there. You learn a new name, then, Thud. Flirts use this to open a conversation, and to tell a bit about themselves. Remember, it's as if you had one chance on "The Dating Game" to reveal a bit about yourself. And the clock is ticking. If you miss this, you miss a golden opportunity.

Introductions fail because after the rigmarole of introductions, the two or more participants realize they have nothing to say to each other. So, before you are introduced, before you stretch out your arm, before you blow this million-dollar opportunity, think of something to add to your introduction, to your "Glad to meet you," to your "Hello." Otherwise you are better off *not* being introduced. Wait.

What happens if you meet someone and blow it? Successful flirts usually are very straightforward. They approach the person again and say: "I'm sorry, but I was so impressed with your handshake, looks, personality, popularity, or cologne [use only one of these] that I don't remember your full name. I'm Karen Smith." He will volunteer his name, and you'll get a second chance. Many successful flirts do this at the end of a party even when they *remember* the name. About that time people are so worn out that they are feeling the same way. (Goodness, I've been here three hours, and I don't remember one person except the guy who bumped into me and spilled my drink.) They're tired of remembering names, and your comment establishes a common bond.

## DRIVING

This requires the prudent use of hand signals. Flirts are big wavers. While driving, they wave to people all over the place. Flirts make a lot of false identifications. "Oh, I thought I knew you. Sorry, your car looked like my ex-girl friend's." (Obviously, he wants to alert you to his breakup.)

A girl friend of mine recently had car trouble on a freeway, so she pulled off at a callbox to telephone for help. Five different men pulled over saying that they thought they recognized her car. Now how is that possible going fifty-five miles per hour? These flirts were proving the other old driving adage. You should always help a damsel or gentleman in distress. However, do this only in daylight and in well-populated areas. Successful flirts aren't stupid. If someone is out of gas, offer to drive to or alert a garage. Should the person look very appealing, you might even bring the gas back yourself. When someone is in an emotional state and in need of your help, they will remember your kind gesture.

## WALKING YOUR DOG

Dogs are not only man's best friend, they are a flirt's best ally. On a Saturday or Sunday afternoon, no one can resist commenting on a good-looking dog. If you really want to attract attention, take your dog not to a park, but to a shopping district. While you can't go in the stores with your Great Dane, he will elicit tons of compliments. Even a miniature poodle can do the trick.

A fabulous flirt I know had her little poodle out on a Saturday and realized she needed a pair of panty hose at one of the large department stores. Very soon a man approached her with the "cute dog" remarks. They got to talking, and she admitted she was in a quandary. Peanuts, her dog, was afraid of the fluorescent lighting in department stores, but she was desperately in need of panty hose. "What! You'd go in and get it for me? Oh, I couldn't ask you to do that. Thanks, very much." She gave him some money, and he returned with money and panty hose, and asked her to have a coffee with him. Naturally she couldn't; Peanuts wouldn't be welcome. And so a date was arranged, all because she needed panty hose.

Men with dogs have an even bigger advantage. Since women

are a bit more reluctant to walk up to a man on the street, the dog acts as a "third party" buffer. Many outrageous women flirts will start talking to the dog. Honest. "Oh, what a good-looking boy. Oh, sorry, girl." Then the conversation leads to, "How long have you had the dog?" "Where does the dog live?" (With you, no kidding?) "Is he alone all day?" (She is? Great. At least there's no little woman at home during the day.)

And another flirting trick for women. Dogs are a great excuse to get home, stay home, or never go out on a date. "I can't leave Sir Lancelot. He's still bothered by thunderstorms." What man would believe that? None. But it's a face-saving way to say no, and good flirts don't hurt people they once flirted with.

## REMOVING YOUR COAT

Ahh! One of the most sensuous, flirtatious actions imaginable. Taking off anything is flirtatious. That's why unbundling at a ski lodge is pure heaven. Stripping away those layers is so seductive.

Women must learn to get out of a jacket or coat without looking like a five-year-old trying to get out of her pajamas. Like models, they must learn how to do this in one continuous, sensual motion. But it needn't be fast. Realize you have all the time in the world. The longer you take, the more you can stretch and maneuver your body into the most unusual (daring!) positions.

Here's how to take your coat off: With both hands flip the lapels and front part of the coat off your shoulders, right hand flipping the right side, left hand flipping the left. The more you practice, the lower this flip lands your coat down your back. Then you extend both arms out in back of you. Now wiggle until the back of the jacket is hanging around your wrists. (This can be really flirtatious. On the other hand, don't overdo; you're just taking off your coat, not your blouse.) Then with your left hand, flick your wrist out of the right side of your coat. With your right hand, do the same with your left wrist, only add a little flourish. (This is what models do.) Do not drag the coat or let it touch the floor. Too tacky. But if you can whisk it up just before it brushes the floor, that is masterful.

For men, do not flip, but shrug the coat off your shoulders.

Then do a combination movement. Push the right arm of the coat down and off your body. Then do the same for the left. In a man's case, efficiency is considered the best course of action. There should be no fumbling, groping for an arm, or pushing and pulling—these make a woman think that you might handle the women in your life in a similar style.

# ♡ 20 ♡
# *Flirtatious Conversations*

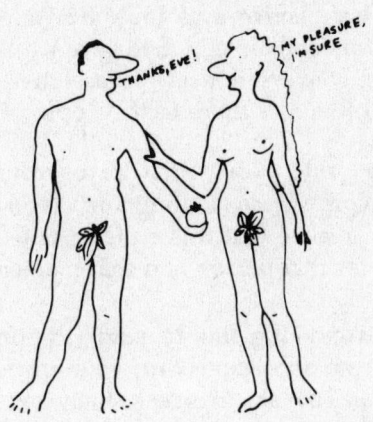

## OPENING LINES

The worst flirting mistake most often takes place in the first sixty seconds of any encounter. And it usually happens when the first person speaks. In flirting, you must remember that our human instincts are to shy away from any stranger, particularly an inquisitive one. Being grilled isn't fun. Who wants to be interrogated by a minor-league Mike Wallace? At least on "60 Minutes," along with the humiliation, you have the glory of being on the top television program.

So save any kind of question that is forceful, probing, or indiscreet for your personal attorney. And make sure there is never any criticism implied in what you say to a new person. Forget things like "What's a nice person like you doing in a place like this?" (Implying that while they are nice, their taste is atrocious.) Or "Couldn't you find anything better to do?" (It's always nice to hear you're slumming.) Or "Haven't we met before?" (At the very least, you're implying that someone's memory is inferior. At best, you are a walking cliché.)

Avoid being too cute, using a funny voice, or trying to tell a joke. But here's the worst: talking to a group of people or a friend loud enough for your prospective flirting partner to overhear that you are talking about him.

Before you utter that first crucial line, here are the rules:

**1. Put on a half smile and look down or avert your gaze.** Looking someone directly in the eye while you are close enough to start a conversation is too assertive. Sure, it will work. But not as often as a more tactful approach.

**2. Forget every rule about what an opening line should be.** If you have a pat phrase, a funny line, an opening that you think is dynamic, realize that this crutch has to go. Anything that isn't created for that person and that moment is suspect.

**3. Adjust your opening line to your flirtatious body language.** If you are an outrageous flirt, your opening lines must compensate for this, so make them especially low key. If you are a low-key flirt, you can be a little more outrageous with your lines. Still, the more conservative you can be, the better.

**4. Opening lines must be about something, but not about the object of your flirtations.** Telling a woman she is beautiful is nice, but it doesn't start an opening conversation. What opening lines must do is elicit further discussion.

Most comments are bland conversation stoppers rather than starters. If you say the band is bad, the food is good, the meeting is long, the class is interesting, you force the listener to think of a response. Should they say the band is good? The class is redundant? Should they agree or disagree? The purpose of your opening line is to stimulate a response, to get a conversation started.

**5. Reveal yourself.** This is the most important thing you can do to make an opening line work. Tell how you are feeling. Opinions should be based on feelings. (Remember, you are flirting, not writing a dissertation for your doctorate in abstract

mathematics.) I feel . . . I think . . . I believe . . . I'm confused
. . . I'm surprised . . . I'm startled . . . I wonder. These are the
phrases to start your opening remarks with time and time
again.

Opening comments must also make the person you are flirting with believe that you are only somewhat accessible. This is
the exact opposite of the power trip most would-be flirts try to
project. At the same time, let your body language show that you
are vulnerable and harmless. In flirting, body language is the
most eloquent language. So when it is coupled with conflicting
verbal suggestions, a person will subconsciously *always* believe
what the body is saying. So set yourself apart from those who
fail while flirting. Flirts who synchronize their body language
of vulnerability and harmlessness with words that show acces-
sibility are the ones who ride off into the sunset with a new
flirting companion each evening. This dual message is irresist-
ible.

So, reveal a flaw. Tell of a fear. Talk about your confusion. All
of these foibles are manna from heaven for flirts.

**6. Ask about something that does not directly relate to your
flirting partner.** Such as: "I feel embarrassed at large gatherings. What is happening on the stage, do you know?" This
opening does three things: It reveals you; it talks about a third
person, object, or subject; and it asks a question. The question
signals the recipient that yes, a response is expected.

Now about the question. If someone can answer with a yes or
no, you have asked the wrong question. Do what talk show
hosts try to do, create an open-ended question. Examples: "I'm
upset about this new account. How would you handle it?" "I'm
always somewhat uncertain at a big party. What's your favorite
type of social event?"

**7. Follow up.** If at first your flirting partner doesn't respond to your disclosure/question, give that person another
chance. Why? Because people aren't always sure how to act at
first. They may be thinking of something else. (Is there a run in
my panty hose? Can she tell I had onion soup for lunch?) And
only if someone is persistently pleasant and conversationally
non-threatening do they answer.

Do venture forth at least twice. Because many flirts have told me that people (even they) are tongue-tied the first time someone speaks to them and kick themselves all the way home for not being more outgoing and friendly.

## FLIRTY CONVERSATIONAL GAMBITS

**Gambit #1.** Flirting requires that you live in the moment. In other words, you don't want to discuss your old landlord, husband, or tennis injuries. Flirtatious conversations are always in the present.

**Gambit #2.** Another tool for the really timid flirt is to talk to a prospective flirting partner as if this person were a brother or sister. But only your words should convey a platonic relationship. Your gestures should be very flirtatious.

**Gambit #3.** In the midst of a flirtatious encounter there are ways to keep your partner interested if you have to leave for a while, or if you want to make sure you will meet again.

Use phrases such as, "Remind me to tell you about my friend who is a Neilsen family." "Well, before you buy that car, talk to me; I know how to get special financing." "I'm talked out right now, but I'll tell you why later." "I really think you should try getting on a game show."

**Gambit #4.** During flirtatious conversations, make sure you talk in short bursts of energy—this replicates the style of lovers. Lovers are also comfortable with silences. So when silence takes over, count to fifty before you say anything. This gets you into an unhurried, intimacy-creating pattern. Styles of flirtatious conversations must follow the pattern that all intimate love relationships take. Why? Because your body and mind relate these rhythms to a romantic cycle in your own life. And your partner does this too. Your romantic memories will be subconsciously triggered; so the more you like someone, the faster you should get into these rhythms.

**Gambit #5.** Observe if your flirting partner's behavior jells with his words. If a woman is talking about her job, but is moving closer, you'd do best to continue this line of discussion

—even if you have to veer the conversation in this direction for a second time. The tip-off is that your partner is moving forward.

Yet if someone is talking about how much his family means to him, which usually is a warm signal, but is leaning back in a chair, fidgeting, repositioning himself away from you, get off the subject and fast. Stay with the issues that draw your partner closer to you physically.

Distance and body language are not "random" noise. Pay attention. Minor movements are critical. Remember, this distance adjustment will not encompass more than a two- to four-inch change in your partner's proximity to you. Yes, inches. But the successful flirt notices these things and acts upon them.

**Gambit #6.** Don't feel you have to make your mark all in one continuous discussion. Most successful flirts structure their flirtatious conversations into small packets. The less you accomplish in the first two or three encounters, the faster the later ones will move in an increasingly pleasant direction. Why? Because people always want what they can't have.

Scandalous flirts use this method. They say hello and smile during the first hour of a party. Then they come back and ask the time or use some other, minor opening line. Then, a third time, a one- or two-phrase repartee takes place. (The flirt asks something. The person answers; the flirt adds a second note. The recipient answers. Then the flirt is gone.)

Or try the "Let's ask Harry" flirting method. Here's how it goes. You and your flirting partner are talking, and you feel a tiny bit of excitement mounting. Do you press your advantage? Do you ask for a phone number? No, you ask for a third opinion. (Just be careful that the person you ask isn't someone who's going to lure your flirting partner away.) Bringing in a third person not only takes the pressure off you, but it throws your partner off-balance. (What is he doing bringing someone else over? Gee, maybe I'll try harder. Or, she was so interested. Was there something wrong with my discussing my carburetor?) Then you should walk away from both people. Anywhere from fifteen minutes to three hours later, you finally return to your flirting partner. But now he is hungry for an explanation, or vindication that he is still interesting and attractive.

# ♡ 21 ♡
# *How to Turn Off a Flirt*
## (Without Blowing Out the Pilot Light)

IT HAPPENS. YOU'VE BEEN FLIRTING FIVE MINUTES OR FIFTY MINUTES OR ALL NIGHT, AND SUDDENLY YOU REALIZE THE FLIRTING HAS TO STOP. Either you are bored; or your partner is taking this encounter too seriously; or you are; or your date suddenly shows up; or you notice something about this person which becomes an instant turn-off; or you think you're going to get stuck for the bar bill; or you consult the I Ching and the timing is wrong; or suddenly all the clues lead you to believe that this person is seriously involved with a friend of yours; or she works for the I.R.S., or he lets it slip that he is going to be a father; or she starts singing, loudly, along with the jukebox. Yes, you need to end this flirtation fast.

But sometimes in the midst of all your brilliantly flirtatious charms, he doesn't get the message, or doesn't want to quit, or a nasty streak emerges. Trouble is brewing.

Naturally you want to avoid this unpleasantness. Immediately try giving your partner a large dose of realism. Here's how this works.

**1. Get the person out of the flirting mode.** You comment on what a great flirt she is, that you've never seen anyone flirt so discreetly but effectively before. You compliment his flirting technique and then ask him how he does it. Talking or addressing his actions makes him focus on them, discontinuing the flirting in the process.

**2. Move into a different light.** Best of all, turn all the lights on, especially if you've been sitting in dim light. Actually any extra voltage will make your partner see you differently.

**3. Leave the room for about twenty minutes.** After about ten or fifteen minutes of waiting, your flirting partner is going to become a little less patient, think you a bit less wonderful, and may even become angry. Upon your return, some of the bloom will be off the rose. So when you suggest you want to visit a friend across the room, your formerly, overly flirtatious partner may be relieved. A trip to the bathroom can serve this purpose. Make sure you come out expressing a rather businesslike attitude, not quite as charming as when you went in, and you'll surely dampen this overly zealous person's spirits.

**4. Join a group.** It's okay if your flirting partner insists on tagging along. But you should focus exclusively on the group. That should tone down the overtures. Try to join a group with both men and women. If you join one of the opposite sex, your flirting partner may encourage the group to make sexual remarks.

**5. Shock your flirting partner.** Say that you smell smoke, hear a siren, hear a doorbell, see someone you recognize from a wanted poster.

**6. Get overly serious.** Don't laugh; don't smile. Say that you want to get down to something that is very important to both of you, the national debt. If you really want to cool matters off permanently, get into a discussion of religion, nihilism, Freud, or the veracity of Margaret Mead's anthropological studies. And don't get off this. Ever. Your partner will try to change the subject, even if he knows something about it. But don't. The less your partner knows, the more you should ramble . . . and ramble . . . and ramble. Continue to discuss it while getting your coat, paying the check, or getting a cab. And never say good-bye directly, just keep talking about the broad ramifications of this vital issue.

Why try these things when you could just as well be rude? You should know by now that good flirts are *never* rude. And for women, it is always better to bore a man than to have him think you were teasing him. The first makes him sleepy; the latter can arouse his sadistic tendencies.

# ♡ IV ♡
# WHEN TO FLIRT

# ♡ 22 ♡
# *Flirting at Work*

SINCE WOMEN BEGAN ENTERING THE WORK FORCE IN THE FIF-
TIES, WORK HAS BECOME THE MOST POTENT APHRODISIAC IMAGIN-
ABLE. This fits in with one of the basic tenets of flirting: Focus
not on your flirting partner or yourself, but upon a third person,
issue, or activity. Work qualifies perfectly.

Flirting at work must still be bound by certain constraints.
You must be able to command respect for your real contribu-
tions on the job, before you start mixing a few flirtatious gestures in with the annual report. But when you feel you have
reached that level of acceptance, the sky's the limit as far as
flirting is concerned.

Flirting is really a great homogenizer. You can flirt with your
secretary as well as a member of the board; you can flirt when
you're with the personnel director and when you're with your
assistant.

In fact, most good male/female working relationships have an
unusual kind of flirting attached to them. Both you and your
colleague express appreciation for one another; that's flirting!
Also, you each have an overview of the situation, meaning that

you both know when your flirting will end. This is called a "flirting cap"; it caps the flirting so that it remains constant, manageable, and unthreatening.

Yet many of you may not want to stifle your flirting. If not, you are best advised to flirt during the non-flirtatious times of the day. Don't flirt at the coffee machine; in fact, by not flirting there, you give your prospective flirting partner a chance to wonder why you have cooled off. Don't flirt at office parties (but all-day seminars were made in heaven for the flirt). And never, ever, flirt going home or riding the elevator to the parking lot. Why not? Everyone does this; besides, it can give people the impression that you are not busy that evening. Although the best flirting times are just when you are leaving the office (5:00 to 7:00 P.M.*), if you leave everyday at that time, it is better to move your office flirting up to 4:00 P.M. and do those little maneuvers with your flirting companion while you are directly in the work environment.

Unless there are special circumstances at play, only flirt at work when you are alone with your flirting partner. Otherwise, the gossip will spread that you like this person. Also, it is best to flirt while the two of you are discussing some big project, problem, or issue. Flirting when he comes by your desk to borrow a paper clip is wasted and may be misinterpreted. At work the rule is: One person flirts at a time. The reciprocal flirting maneuver should take place at a new time and place.

---

*These are the "bewitching hours," when people are starting to think about their personal lives but are not yet deadly serious about the social whirl. This is when you can catch your flirting partners off guard!

# ♡ 23 ♡
# *The Multiple Uses of the Business Card*

BUSINESS CARDS ARE INVALUABLE FOR SUCCESSFUL FLIRTS. They endow you with cachet and style that sets you apart from would-be flirts and imposters. They give you a more professional, worldly image. A business card tells everyone that, yes, you expect others will want to contact you, and because of the *numerous* requests you've had in the past, you've decided it would be easier to have something printed up with all the information.

But what if you aren't in business? What if you are a student, homemaker, traveler, heiress, secretary, bus driver, policeman, or sanitation worker? Why on earth would you need a business card? Because you are a flirt. And flirts know that it doesn't do them any good at all to flirt with someone they'd like to know better, if the person forgets their name. Or doesn't have paper to write down a number, or is embarrassed to ask how to reach them.

No, you do not give out your cards indiscriminately. But when someone asks for your phone number, how to spell your name, or a scrap of paper to write down something—Ah! Perfection. You donate your card as the writing material.

What should be on your card? If you are married, just your name, probably just your first name. If you are not married, you should include your full name, printed in the middle of the card. Most flirts print a telephone number in the right-hand corner. But some women don't want to include this because they change it so often, or are cautious. If this is the case, just have your name printed. Then, pen at the ready, you can say, "Let me put my special phone number down for you." This is so flirtatious, even if you are living out of a phone booth at Penn Station.

If you do print a phone number on your card, you might make it a work number, or an answering-service number; you do have to provide a way for someone to get in touch with you. Never, ever, include your address. Your flirting partner doesn't get that until you know him or her better. Remember, keep something in reserve.

Don't think that you have to put the name of a company or your occupation on a card. Even some business people with very impressive titles and jobs have social cards like these printed up. As one female television executive told me, "I don't want some man calling me up because he wants to become a newscaster. I want a man to call because I looked fabulously attractive." But some flirts feel differently. A man said, "Sure, I use my position. All flirts use every asset they have. I've worked hard to get where I am, neglecting the emotional side of life. Now I'm going to use this position to help me become a more balanced person."

Print up the fewest cards your printer will allow the first time. After using them a while you'll probably realize there's something about the card that just isn't you. You might add an office address, a new phone number, a new name, or even a saying (tread lightly here; this can be a turn-off). And what can you do with old cards? Nothing. Even the Salvation Army can't use them.

# ♡ 24 ♡
# *The Traveling Flirt*

HAVE YOU OFTEN THOUGHT ABOUT INDULGING IN A BIT OF FLIRTING, BUT WERE AFRAID THAT SOMEONE WOULD SEE? And worse, perhaps see you fail in your flirtatious approach? Well, that's why a man invented travel. Travel under the guise of business (called hunting and berry-gathering in the old days) is something special. We know it. Why? It makes us less inhibited.

As one successful flirt told me, "As soon as I get on a plane, I feel suddenly very flirtatious. Even though I have a boyfriend, being on my own makes me feel lighter and happier. And the lifted restrictions make me act and appear more approachable."

I have a flirtatious woman friend who swears by traveling. She says she always meets someone. And she does. Not just someone who she talks with, but someone who calls her and tries to see her on a continuing basis. What makes this so romantic? The uncertainty. Both the thrill and the fear of the unknown—the meat and potatoes of any flirting atmosphere.

All the rituals attendant to traveling are so romantic. Leaving someone at an airport, picking them up. I knew a flirtatious man who, whenever a relationship wasn't going well, would tell his girl friend he had to go away for a quick sales trip. She would take him to the airport and see him off. He would wait ten minutes and take a cab back home.

Then there's the flirtatious "collect" call. (The telephone company has tried to end these by inventing credit cards. Don't let them get away with this romance dampener.) Flirts know that placing and accepting a collect call creates a special bond between two people. Frankly I always "forget" my credit card number, and so should you.

Now when you're traveling, you needn't be as flirtatious as

you are at other times, but you do need to communicate more than usual. Ask to share a cab, ask where the best shopping districts are, how to find another airline, when the bars open and close, how far it is to town. Ask about the major business of the region, the weather forecast, the best place to eat. People love to volunteer information. Sure, you'll have bad luck sometimes and get stuck to the one person on the plane who wants to sleep, snore, and ignore you. But on a 747, there is always someone who will catch your eye, if you really try. Which brings us to the rules:

1. **Put yourself in a peopled environment.** Try to get on the largest plane or the busiest commuter train, plane, or bus. Get the limousine service to the airport from your hotel.

In that environment, you chat. You find out about the person next to you, you ask someone to reach up and get you a blanket, you talk to those registering at your hotel. Again, since everyone else wants to connect with someone, you'll find that at least one person out of ten will turn out to be a lucky connection.

2. **Planes—on board and off.** For women, the best place to meet men, other than on board, is at the luggage pick-up. Or else at the car rental counter.

Men have it even easier. Let's face it, most women travel with way too much carry-on luggage. Ask to carry it for her. She'll be forced by the blisters on her hands to accept, and because she wants you to keep carrying it to the door, she'll start up the conversation. Easy.

3. **At hotels, stay away from the lobby.** But do make multiple visits to the newspaper stand. For women flirts, going to pick up the paper between 6:00 and 7:30 A.M. should net you more than the early news. Male flirts will have their best luck around 10:00 to 11:00 A.M. in either the coffee shop or around the bell captain's desk.

4. **If you are traveling by car, go to the garage yourself to pick up your car.** Why? You'll be much more likely to find flirting partners that way. Couples will ask for a car to be brought around, but usually those traveling alone are in more of

a hurry, less patient, and more inclined to do the driving themselves.

**5. The best part of any trip. Your return.** What, no one is waiting for you? Then call them up and invite them over. Spending five minutes telling twenty friends about your adventures with the waif on the street in Hong Kong will either deplete your libido or bring you several invitations for a home-cooked or good old American dinner out.

**6. And if nothing at all happened on your trip.** You signed the contract, made the deal, saw the person you had to see. But that was all? Don't mention the lack of social benefits. Just smile when someone asks about what "else" you did. Mystery brings out the imagination in us all. And your flirting partner will assume that you had the kind of time you secretly wish you had had.

# ♡ 25 ♡
# *Flirting with Food*

JUST LIKE EATING WITH MOM, EATING TOGETHER WITH SOME-
ONE PRODUCES A KIND OF "COMFORT" ZONE. After all, can you
eat when you're scared or unhappy? (Sure you can. But usually,
under those conditions, it isn't called eating, it's called binging,
and you do it alone.) So eating is a very flirtatious gesture. If
you want it to be.

The basics. Yes, you'll have to be mannerly on the first few
outings. People are conditioned by society and their elderly
aunts to be turned off by slovenly behavior at the table. It is
gross to be gross while eating. So if in doubt, don't do it, don't
eat it, and, better yet, don't order it. Wait and grab an ice cream
cone on the way home.

When eating with someone, do not order food you aren't
absolutely certain you know how to eat. Stay away from food
that can get caught in your teeth. Also avoid fried chicken, corn
on the cob, garlic bread, ribs, and spaghetti (unless you are
absolutely sure how to twist the pasta).

Finger foods are excellent when flirting and usually show up
at parties. The reason they are so flirtatious is that you can take
a bite, chew, and then wait a minute before nibbling at this
morsel once again with your very appealing lips. Of course, ice
cream, yogurt, popsicles, popcorn, and fruit are also quite suit-
able.

Women are right when they counsel their women friends not
to eat a lot on the first date. This isn't because men will assume
they are gluttons, as women fear, but rather because men seem
to find it disconcerting to have a woman spend all her time over
some scallops instead of listening to them.

Female flirts suggest that men check their beards and mustaches every few minutes, since food caught there is absolutely

horrid. Women like men who care about food and eating, as this signifies they are sensuous beings. They really like it when men overindulge. And when a man orders dessert instead of fussing about how it is bad for him and you, it's a good sign that he is warm and friendly.

One warning about eating: A man or woman who becomes irate if you eat in their car ("You'll get the floor mats dirty!") is not someone you want to spend the rest of your life with. (Think how fussy they'll be about the towels you leave on the floor!) Though it's not very flirtatious to eat while being driven by a flirting partner, you ought to test your chauffeur's level of tolerance, just for future reference.

# ♡ 26 ♡
## *Flirtatious Drinks*

THERE IS NO BETTER ACCESSORY AT A PARTY THAN A GLASS IN YOUR HAND. It gives your hands something to do, which has a calming effect. Then you have to put the glass down, freshen it up, get a napkin. The activities surrounding drinking are a flirting ritual of themselves. Still there are guidelines for making the most of your opportunities to flirt while enjoying your liquid refreshment.

(FEMALE)   (MALE)

1.   **Never refer to it as your "liquid refreshment" or any other cute name.** This makes others question if you might not already have sampled a bit too much of the brew.

2.   **For women flirts, a straw is one of the best accessories imaginable.** You can twirl it or dip it, but for goodness sake, don't take it out in what pseudo-flirts call a bold motion. This is juvenile and not very flirtatious.

3.   **For men, it is best not to gulp a drink or down it quickly. And never order anything with an umbrella in it.** If by mistake you do get the umbrella, put it and the fruit aside immediately. But, all is not lost. You might offer them to your female flirting partner—this is considered by women to be a nice, friendly gesture. Male flirts say that though women can

drink those overly gimmicky drinks, sometimes considered ultra-feminine, men should stay away.

**4. If you are ever in a place that serves free champagne, order a regular drink from the menu.** This sets you apart. You're not one of the people who are eating a tasteless brunch just so you can sip all that free, cheap champagne.

**5. Long, cool drinks are flirtatious.** So is anything that can be stirred or mixed or shaken. This implies that you are going to be there for a while, which helps take the pressure off the situation. (If you were in a hurry, you'd decide on something that the bartender could make faster.) Giving a hurried appearance is never a good idea. Better to order something complicated and not drink it all, if you are serious about flirting.

**6. All kinds of frothy drinks or drinks in frosted glasses are flirtatious.** As is anything that comes in a huge glass. The one exception is beer.

**7. Drinking beer out of a gigantic mug is out.** This is definitely not flirtatious for women for two reasons: Women look like weight lifters when they lift the mug, and a gigantic mug doesn't give a man an opening to offer a drink. (Why should he? You have enough there for the whole evening.) Successful women flirts never order pitchers or regular bottles of wine for that reason. However, a half bottle is always flirtatious, both for men and women.

Male flirts who drink beer should never put a two-quart pitcher on the table because it acts as a psychological barrier when women approach. And men who drink beer are sexier and more appealing drinking it out of a glass. But if glasses aren't available, cans are certainly more flirtatious than bottles.

**8. Flirts of both sexes should stay away from short drinks.** And particularly stay away from having a shot of anything. (What's your hurry?) But wine is always good. It implies a bit of culture—a plus in every way! It depicts you as a social person, and since it goes so fast, it's easy to finesse a refill. Getting a refill either from the host, bartender, or your drinking partner can be an occasion to talk, touch, and share something.

**9.   Bring Your Own Booze and Pour Your Own Drink parties are really very flirtatious.**   Why? This gives all the guests control over how much, what, and when they drink. It makes everyone a party contributor.

**10.   Should a man offer to buy a woman a drink? Yes.** However, grab your seats because the reverse is *not* true. Though a man may profess to love it when a woman offers him a drink, this flirtatious gesture usually hurts a woman's chances for any kind of a normal, respectful relationship. A woman who brings wine or an after-dinner liqueur over to a man's home as a present, however, is considered not only flirtatious, but warm, caring, and definitely wife material.

**11.   Teetotalers can be just as flirtatious as anyone by drinking soda.**   But do keep drinking along with the others. Every group needs someone who's sober enough to drive them all home.

# ♡ 27 ♡
# *Flirting with Pictures*

ONE PICTURE IS WORTH A THOUSAND FLIRTATIOUS GESTURES, BECAUSE IT *CREATES* THEM. With cameras and pictures, you can do the nearly impossible. You can draw attention to yourself by paying attention to others.

**Stage One: Your camera.** Even if you have no film in it, a camera is almost as good as a dog for attracting random comments from strangers. And the strap—only a born flirt would think of putting a flirtatious strap on photographic equipment. But it's there, so use it. Whip the camera around your neck and off your shoulders. Put it into a bag, set it down, fiddle with it, shake it, finger it, toy with it, ahh . . . this is a flirting prop extraordinaire.

**Stage Two: Consider using it.** Do yourself a favor. Get a Polaroid at first. Is this flirtatious? You bet. Proof positive is the fact that even little old ladies on vacation bring a Polaroid so they can have something to give the natives on their travels. Well, give your "natives" something, too. Also having a Polaroid helps you graduate into . . . .

**Stage Three: Get a camera that demands you develop the film.** And it's best if you tell your flirting partner that those one-hour shops won't do your camera work justice. (You don't have to be a great photographer. Just someone who appears to have a *real interest* in photography. That way no one will suggest you have a *machine* develop your creations. And if your flirting partner is the least bit vain, tell him or her that those fast-developing places really mess up the skin tones, making you look either ghostly pale or so dark even your own mother wouldn't recognize you.) Why not use a fast place? Because after you take some pictures of the person(s) you are flirting with, you will want an excuse to see them again.

A male flirt, a businessman who has graced the covers of several national magazines, once went gaga over a woman flirt who took some candids of him as he was tying up his sailboat. Could he get copies? Could he get in touch with her tomorrow? When would they be ready? And this from a man who is usually blasé about superficial things. But not photos of himself.

Women must be careful when photographing not to admire the physical features of a man too openly. This often forces the conversation toward a more sexual direction. However, male flirts who admire a woman's non-sexual features will come a-cross quite well.

There are, of course, the more subtle manuevers associated with your camera flirting. Like photographing a prospective flirt's children or his pet or his friend. The latter is so effective. Who would guess who you are really after? Then you can ask the opinion of the friend (your real flirting objective). You and he become instant buddies as you work to photograph his friend.

**Stage Four: Get your partner to use it.** Ask your prospective flirting companion to take a picture of you or one of you and a friend. Then you'll have a chance to get near your prospective flirting companion to *explain* your camera, its quirks, your bad side, the way you want the picture framed. Sometimes you may take so many pictures that it is too costly to develop them. So what? Film is cheap compared to the processing costs. So shoot away and then discard. Should he get in touch with you (because you were so delightful) and ask to see the pictures you can say, "Oh, no! They didn't come out." (Of course they didn't. You didn't even send them in!) He will just have to do it all again. Thus more contact, and a bona fide flirting success.

# ♡ 28 ♡
# *When* Not *to Flirt*

THERE ARE TIMES NOT TO FLIRT. When you're sick. When you're with your children. When you're on the witness stand. On second thought, you probably could flirt at these times. People would be off guard.

But you should never flirt when you feel you have to: If you must get a date for the weekend; if you want to impress your best friend; if you're tired. Flirting requires that you have other

things on your agenda, pleasant things that are probably *more* important than flirting. Should flirting become all important, you're at an immediate disadvantage. Because all your energies will be tied to flirting. Sadly, it won't work. This can lead to a negative flirting cycle, which, like all habits, is hard to break.

Of course, you'd never flirt with the husband or wife or even the lover of a friend. (Not nice.) You'd never flirt with someone you instinctively don't trust. (Not safe.) And, you'd never flirt with your mail carrier. (Mail service is bad enough without having everyone flirt with the postal employees.)

Are there any other circumstances where you shouldn't flirt? At family reunions. Things are difficult enough with all the complications brought about by stepfamilies. Flirting here is a waste. You should instead be preparing the turkey or fixing the potato salad. That's what good flirts do when they are among their relatives at a special family event.

# ♡ V ♡
# WHERE TO FLIRT

# ♡ 29 ♡
# *Flirting Haunts*

JUST AS FLOWERS ATTRACT BEES, SO FLIRTS CAN ATTRACT FAVOR-ABLE NOTICE WHEN THEY PUT THEMSELVES IN THE RIGHT ENVIRON-MENT. It makes no sense to be looking your best and ready to flirt if you are fishing in the woods. Forget the movies; people have enough trouble finding seats, they'll never notice you. Video arcades and malls are out. People are too busy remembering where they parked their cars to pay any attention to you. And leave the early morning walks to married folks who want some time alone. Do as successful flirts do. Put yourself where the action is; here are some of the best current places.

**1. Political Action Groups, Committees, or Organizations.** These emotional cauldrons are the mother's milk of flirting. People are excited. They care a lot. And how busy can they be if they have time to attend all these meetings? Flirting here must be a bit bolder than usual because everyone's doing it. Style and originality, as well as who you know, can add immeasurably to your clout. The best flirting goes on during the last nine weeks of any campaign (the crucial period), which is plenty of time to flirt with any one gang.

You could also collect petitions. Stand on the street with a pal to show you are not up to something. Set up a card table and chairs. Flirters know that those little card tables are to flirts what khaki is to the army. Camouflage. Get a cause and move on it.

If you live in a big city where you just can't set up your little table, then find out when the next demonstration is (for a cause you're not embarrassed to believe in), and march.

**2. Video Cassette Rental Stores.** Invented by someone who loves both movies and flirting. The best time to go in is

Thursday evening and late Sunday night. Thursday is when cassettes are most likely to be picked up, and Sunday is when they'll be returned. At about ten o'clock on Sunday night, look for a single, solitary soul trying to save one day's rental at the store, and you've spotted a real romantic candidate.

Avoid Friday and Saturday evenings, but the afternoons and mornings on those days are fine.

**3. Computer Stores.** Since no one understands these things, all you need do is spot someone you like and ask how he managed to understand the computer. Most will say that they haven't quite mastered it. So . . . you can learn together. If he has learned already, you'll immediately fall into a natural (flirtatious) conversation in which you are instructed on how to deal with BASIC. People rarely think to flirt here, because it is such a sterile environment. But those who have swear by this virtual treasure trove of untapped flirting partners.

**4. Supermarkets.** Especially the under-ten-items check-out lines. Here are the people who don't think further ahead than Tuesday. Meaning that there are many things up in the air in their lives, probably including their relationships. Flirting here provides two real bonuses. You have to flirt quickly, and based on a time investment of only five minutes, you both can decide whether or not to continue the relationship.

Another great flirting area of the supermarket is the fresh produce department. Half the people there don't understand how to cook the stuff they buy; the other half does. Figure out which group you're in and start flirting with the other. It's never inappropriate to ask someone how to steam cauliflower or artichokes. And if someone thinks you are flirting just turn to another person and ask a second question, totally throwing your prospective flirt off balance.

**5. Seminars.** The perfect combination: a third party or subject focus, common interests, and a chance to flirt. If your company will pay or contribute to the costs, take as many seminars as you can. These are hotbeds of romance. And the fact that you're all attending the same seminar has already helped you preselect your flirting partner.

**6. Night Schools.** Good but not as great as everyone thinks. Better to attend one-shot lectures. Weekend courses are much more suited for flirting. If you want to use a university or college as your flirting base, head for the research libraries and the specialized archives. This is slower than other methods, but can produce some real flirting treasures.

**7. TV and Video Repair Shops.** The tools of modern civilization always break down, and flirts use these minor discomforts as opportunities to find new partners. Or at least to have a good time while they wait to get an estimate. Ask opinions of others while you are waiting. Do not go at a slow time. (You're flirting, aren't you?) Choose lunch hours or Saturday mornings to haul your set to the shop.

**8. Newsstands.** A neighborhood newsstand can be your flirting oasis. Just make sure you become friendly enough with the owners so that they allow you to linger and read some of the magazines. Saturdays and Sundays are best here. And Sunday morning is a prime time for finding a new flirting partner who may have long-term potential.

**9. Car Washes.** The ideal day is Saturday. And midday is best. Most of the people are getting their cars clean for the weekend, to impress someone of the opposite sex that night. But don't let that bog you down; they're still out there and ready to flirt. And these are people who obviously make an effort for a date. Prime flirting material. Never go on ladies' day or men's day. What for? If all you wanted was a clean car you could use your hose.

**10. Take-Out Food Places.** But only at lunchtime. Only. At that time, people are hustling and bustling. They are busy, but alas they do have to wait for their orders to be made up. That's where you flirts do the establishment and their customers a world of good. You provide a sociable atmosphere. You know the people you meet here are responsible (they're hurrying back to the office, aren't they?) and you might also see them a couple of times before you make your move. You should never take a table while you wait. Wander, instead. This gives you more flirting flexibility.

**11.  Office Furniture and Stationery Supply Stores.**  The best flirting zone is near the calendar section from December to January. Everyone needs a calender book, right? Even people who have secretaries like to select their own date books. So there you are, perusing the selections. At other times of the year, you can also easily meet people here. Ask questions. "Do these labels work with a Xerox machine?" Or, "Can you get refills for this book?" Anything. But a word to save you time, expense, and heartbreak. Flirting in a regular furniture store is usually worthless. Most people shopping there have a friend in tow, who is helping them make "their" selections. But if you must, men seem to have much better flirting luck in furniture stores than women.

**12.  The Sierra Club.**  Wasn't this started as an organization to bring people in the West—socially isolated because of the great distances—together? I think so. Well, it's expanded its purpose. Now they do all kinds of things like saving birds and trees and making sure the wilderness still has enough snakes to scare off city folk who want to litter the great outdoors. But that isn't all.

They have special hikes, trips, lectures, and all sorts of activities for people whose skin needs exposure to ultraviolet, and not fluorescent, lighting. So call; join. You'll never see such an attractive group of flirts trooping around in hunting boots.

**13.  Religious Organizations.**  They are back in vogue, and are really responding to the growing single and liberated populations. Socializing has become one of the tools they use to attract new members. In fact, there are so many flirts at these gatherings, that one minister told me, all he needs to do is get a few warm and friendly men and women (we call them flirts), and his church membership jumps 100 percent. And most religious groups aggressively go after new members by trying to fill the community's need for a meeting ground. Naturally you're going to want to shop around for the organization that fits your moral and social needs, but you'll find one. Don't bypass this.

**14.  Sporting Goods Stores.**  On weekends and evenings

these stores are populated by active men and women who are just waiting for you to flirt. Look, they are spending all their money on equipment so they can ski, surf, scuba dive, or ride, and one of the purposes of those activities is to meet someone. Flirting at a sporting goods store saves your prospective flirting recipient from going out and doing all those difficult activities. What a break! And you'll save them so much money in the process. Best times to go are during the big athletic seasons, when skiing, hiking, and swimming are popular. For women: Make sure you don't bother going to these stores during a major football or baseball game, as they will be empty.

**15. Hobby Shops.** Stores that sell photographic equipment, paints, art supplies, and (best of all) stereo equipment are flirting heaven.

As for stereo equipment stores, go when they are having a sale (more people). Since the sales force will be overoccupied, you'll be able to flirt by asking for help and advice and by testing the equipment. Saturday mornings are best here. As for the other hobby shops, after 6:00 P.M. is best, so go on Wednesday and Thursday evenings when they stay open late.

**16. Travel Agencies.** Go during the busiest times. Lunch hour is ideal. And choose your travel agency based on location. Hotels are good, but best of all are travel agencies on the ground floor of a huge office building (a lot of foot traffic). You'll have men and women visiting who not only want to go to Tahiti for a week, but who have to travel to Tokyo for a trade show. Always pick up your airline tickets here—it takes a bit longer but provides multiple flirting opportunities.

**17. Athletic Activities with Tournaments, et cetera.** Just being seen wearing your snazzy outdoor clothes makes you appear accessible. Offer to help with the tournament if you're able. It takes guts to show up alone; so bring a friend. Tournaments are one place where you'll do better flirting if you are with someone else.

**18. Bars with Big-Screen TVs.** How many people want to put one of those ugly projecting devices in the middle of their living rooms and spend $4000.00 in the process? Few! So you and all the other sports, movies, and special-events buffs congregate at the big screen. This gives you the perfect reason for being at a bar, instead of at home. And since you are all focusing on the program, the flirting atmosphere is a bit more restrained and more conducive to flirting than regular bars.

**19. Xerox and Paper Copying Places.** Don't you have to copy your report, a check, a receipt? Sure you do, and so does everyone else in the world. Copy places thrive just before April 15. If possible, do all the copying yourself. The fact that you are playing with the machine, figuring it out, gives you something to do, and invites comments from others. (For a change let them do the flirting.)

**20. Dry Cleaners.** Go at the busiest times, from 5:00 to 7:00 P.M. and on mid-Saturday morning. Choose one that has twenty-four-hour service; successful flirts say that this attracts the kind of dynamic people (What, my blue suit isn't clean? I have to wear it at my job interview tomorrow morning) who will respond to your flirting. If you want someone who's a bit low key, try those do-it-yourself tumblers. But your clothes will look better, and you'll have a more attractive partner on your arm, if you stick to the professional dry cleaners.

# ♡ 30 ♡
# *Flirting at the Salad Bar*

SINCE SALAD BARS ARE THE NEW FLIRTATIOUS GATHERING SPOTS, HERE IS A DIGEST IN SALAD-BAR HOPPING.

The most important things to remember are: Don't overload your plate; don't use the coarsely ground pepper, as it will end up wedged between your teeth and look like an ugly cavity; and don't put any cherry tomatoes on your salad. They usually end up splattered on your clothing. Save cherry tomatoes for when you are home, nude, or both.

Other tips for salad-bar hoppers:

**Rule #1:** Keep your salad plate looking bland, that way no one will be offended by what you take.

**Rule #2:** The second-helping syndrome. If you fill up your plate too soon—you'll loose a good reason for going back to the salad bar.

**Rule #3:** In line, get ahead of the person you'd like to flirt with. Then while he is trying to stab an ornery vegetable—you scoop it up and put it onto his plate.

**Rule #4:** In selecting your greens, be aware that you can tell a lot about someone by their preferred salad makings. *Example:* Find a woman with only iceberg lettuce, and you've found someone who's as "cold" as the lettuce. Boston lettuce signifies a rather fussy person. Endive is the salad green of the sexual critic; while red-leaf lettuce means that the person cares more about appearances than substance. The best choice is a bit of everything, although the salad should not be piled like a bale of hay, but sprinkled over the plate.

Then there is the person who goes down the salad bar backwards. First the onions; then the tomatoes, artichokes, and cucumbers; then the green beens and olives; and finally the lettuce. This would be sexy except that they have usually depleted the supply of the specialties, angering just about everyone else in the line.

Backwards-salad-bar-hoppers are apt to cheat while married, though they are usually faithful while you are dating. These people are not a romantic best-bet.

**Rule #5:** It is not flirtatious to discuss the hygiene standards of the restaurant while waiting for the person ahead of you to select their mushrooms. Let the look of the guacamole drive this point home for you.

**Rule #6:** The closer your plate of salad fixings matches the one of your desired flirting partner, the sooner this person will warm up to you.

**Rule #7:** Flirts know that beets can turn your tongue red, mint jelly can turn it green; and both of these colors can turn a prospective flirting partner off.

**Rule #8:** Never get crudités. Chomping on them is far too noisy. What are your chances of someone falling for you because of the distinctive sound you made when you ground down your zucchini?

# ♡ 31 ♡
# *Flirting at Parties*

IF YOU GO TO A PARTY AND REALIZE YOU DON'T KNOW ANYONE, YOU CAN EITHER DECIDE TO LEAVE OR YOU CAN REGARD IT AS A MARVELOUS OPPORTUNITY TO TEST YOUR FLIRTING AND FRIENDSHIP SKILLS. After all, most of these people are like you; they went to this party to meet new people. So by going out of your way to flirt, you are actually making the party more of a success for them.

Here's how to start.

1. **Survey the group.** This is not the time to flirt, but to plan. Get a drink or a sandwich and sit down. Watch those who seem to be the king or queen pins. Look around and you'll see other people who seem lost. Note those people with dates, particularly those dates who seem to be listening a lot and not joining the conversation.

2. **Assume that everyone is socially nervous.** Therefore, they may not be at their most courteous. Why? Anxiety breeds nervous reactions and fear, two things that bring out the worst in people. So, as you introduce yourself to people, tell them your connection to the party. "I'm a friend of Peter and Jane, and they mention you all the time." Do anything you can to put them at ease, so they will present the best side of themselves to you.

3. **Don't flirt until you know the atmosphere.**

4. **Pass the food or offer to help serve the buffet.**

5. **Ask for help moving the chairs, looking for a lost bracelet, or organizing a game or social activity.**

**6. Now you can start flirting.** First go for the people who seem unsure of themselves. Talk to them; form your own group. You can even play matchmaker for two people who seem lost. By doing this you compliment the man or woman for his/her sex appeal, and you extend friendship to the person of your same sex.

**7. Dance.** Yes, it's corny and old-fashioned, but there is no better way to flirt than to dance your head off in a party atmosphere. People will look at you, and those who like to dance will be more inclined to talk with you. If you are really good, you can show your cute new friend how to do something. And here's the bonus payoff. When you are a terrific dancer and you stop dancing to talk to (flirt with!) someone, that person feels doubly special. With all your talent and love of music, you have chosen to be with them. This alone could ensure your success for the evening.

**8. Bring the records, tapes, or video tapes.** Be the person responsible for the background entertainment. That way you can flit from person to person asking what they would like to see or hear, and then, quite naturally, stay at the side of the person who interests you. Since music requires continual monitoring, you can go back several times with a perfectly logical excuse, and suddenly you are part of a group—an important part at that.

**9. At BYOB parties, bring rosé wine.** Since no one drinks rosé wine, it will still be unopened at the end of the evening. You flirts can then present it to the man or woman you are trying to impress, saying, "Try this at home, and let me know if you like it." To make this appear spontaneous, do not write your telephone number on the label ahead of time; instead put it in crayon on the bottom of the bottle.

## EMERGENCY MEASURES

**1. Find another single person.** And start talking about something that always brings a strong response: abortion, politics, busing, education, taxes, A.I.D.S. When others sense the discussion, they'll join in. People love to air their views, especially when someone has already introduced the subject. This will attract attention, and you can then zero in on whomever you like, by asking her opinion. Since you are the ringleader, it is natural and unthreatening for you to take the lead.

**2. Disappear.** If you are having a rotten time, sit in the bathroom or the bedroom or the hall. Then, when the party is about one hour old (yes, it takes this long), return. People will ask where you were. Or they will think you are a new guest, and since they are bored with the people they've been talking with for an hour, you will seem novel and thus appealing.

**3. Telephone a friend.** If you have a telephone credit card, make it long distance. This way you fix two problems—you make necessary calls and you give yourself a break from the depressing mood the party has put you in. Right in the middle of your misery, talking to your mother may not seem that bad. Or, call a friend and explain how you are feeling. They may cheer you up with good news or simply renew your confidence. This will lighten your mood, which, in turn, will attract new friends.

**4. Call the local phone number that gives you the update on sports scores or the latest news.** If your city doesn't have one and you are really desperate, call the local all-news radio or television station and ask them the scores or their lead news item. Now return to the party with this information. Do it with flair; make an announcement. Scores always attract people and contribute to a new conversation bent. If this is a particularly ritzy (read, pretentious) group, announce the latest economic, foreign, or political happenings.

**5. Leave.** Yes, leave. Keep one good book at home that you are dying to read, so you can really look forward to doing this. Of course, if you have tried #4, announced your "news" and got no reaction, you can make it seem as if you must leave because of it. Notice how you suddenly seem desirable. If that happens, throw caution to the winds, and approach the most desirable person there (besides yourself), and say, "I have to run, but there was something I wanted to talk to you about. Where can I reach you?" Usually they'll let you know. Should this person suddenly be joined by a date, quickly get the number, then say to them both, "I'll tell you about it sometime next week. I've got to run." This takes both you and your prospective new friend off the hook.

Remember to make a thank-you call to the host or hostess. You might carefully steer the conversation to the subject of that gorgeous redhead or that handsome stockbroker. Where can you get in touch with them? Your host won't ask why. Because one of the best ways you can compliment a partygiver is to acknowledge what an attractive, desirable group of people their gathering drew. They won't find anything strange about your liking their other guests; they assumed you would, or you wouldn't have been invited.

Keep in mind the one out of ten rule. For the average person only one out of ten social or business events, activities, or introductions works out. If this one didn't, so what? At least you only have nine more to go.

# ♡ 32 ♡
# *Flirting and Fitness*

FITNESS IS THE GODMOTHER OF FLIRTING. It fits all the criteria. It puts you in touch with your body; thus, with your feelings. You are not worried about impressing someone else because you are completely into your exercising. And it puts you in close, very close, proximity to people. This continued non-verbal contact is so reassuring that no one is the least taken aback when you start talking. And you can start talking about the most personal thing: your body. How fetching.

Flagrant flirts say you should always attend your fitness club around 7:00 A.M. or after 7:00 P.M. in the evening. On weekends, you'll do best on Sunday afternoons. People at health clubs during these hours seem to have more free time, more flexible schedules—important if you want them to respond to your flirting. Do you want someone who has to get home for a babysitter because her husband is working the weekend shift? No. Family times become flirting times, because that's when all the most promising flirting partners show up. The others are home watching television with their families.

The location of the club is important. You should always join one in the city. City people are in more of a mood to flirt. In the suburbs, all they want to talk about is the cost of a mortgage. (Presumably they've just bought their dream cottage, without you.) Clubs with lots of weekend sports competitions are best. While you are revving up for your handball championship, you might as well be in the most alluring atmosphere you can find. Then when you win, people will have an excuse to come up and talk to (congratulate) you.

Successful flirts say there is one unbeatable location in any health or fitness facility—the coed saunas, spas, massage tables (the best!), and whirlpool. If you can cozy up to a pro-

spective flirting partner and get them to confide their problems and thoughts to you while their little pores open, you will have developed more than just a relationship. You'll have a special bond.

Some sociologists suggest that the hot temperatures replicate the warmth and protective environment of the womb. (You were in a symbiotic relationship with your mom, remember.) And the rocking motion associated with pressured water massages or normal massages reactivates the memory of this emotional massage. Then your flirting partner associates these warm feelings with you. You are kind and solicitous. You are putting your best foot, side, or thigh forward. If thousands of years of civilization couldn't extinguish this primeval urge to bond with someone you feel comfortable with, you should play it for all it's worth.

One other benefit. Your flirting partner attributes his lazy, relaxed feelings to you.

Like skiers who prefer the après-ski life to the lift lines, fitness devotees who stay for more than a few minutes at the juice bars are asking to have their "intentions" questioned. ("Why is he spending so much time nursing a grapefruit juice?" or "She's just a snow bunny.") This sort of lingering should be avoided by a flirt; it's far too obvious. So if you must wait for someone, do it in the locker rooms or stay a while longer at the aerobics class.

Dance, aerobics, and jazz exercise classes are now coed. But unless there is a huge class and the group you've joined is special for some reason, health clubs are considered better places to flirt. Watching someone do a tummy tuck day after day is not as flirtatious as seeing them lift weights. Also, at a health club you make your own routine, and there is more individual activity which encourages talk. And the informality is a plus.

But what if you like your body just the way it is—ten pounds overweight? Where do you meet your physical counterpart? Just go to any of the foot, knee, or orthopedic clinics at the local hospital. They are filled with weekend athletes who have over-exercised and hurt themselves. And naturally since they're out of shape (the injury!), they'll like the more sedentary things you do. The best time to flirt at these clinics is late Sunday night and early Monday morning, when the seriousness of the injuries these weekend athletes have suffered becomes apparent.

In case you really hate to do all these athletic things, the secret underground movement may be for you. It is for everyone who would rather see a movie, sit on the beach, enjoy an all-day brunch, read, hold hands, or make love, than go through the rigmarole of working out, sweating, showering, dressing, and then falling asleep from the exertion. You won't find these people at health clubs; you'll find them at vitamin stores, die-tetic candy shops, salad bars (getting the second helpings), and at the post office huddled over their private, post office box. Why? These people are no exceptions. They want to be thin and gorgeous too, but they prefer to send for those mysterious weight-loss diets through the mail. That way they can combine a trip to the post office with some flirting, and pick up the pie on the way home.

# ♡ 33 ♡
# *Creating a Flirtatious Environment*

BEFORE YOU TRY TO LOWER THE LIGHTS, PROGRAM YOUR TAPES TO PLAY ROMANTIC MUSIC, AND GIVE YOUR CAT HIS SUPPER SO HE'LL SLEEP FOR FIVE HOURS; DO THE THINGS THAT WILL REALLY MAKE THE FLIRTATIOUS DIFFERENCE.

## AT HOME

1. **Make a cozy environment.**

2. **Have a cozy place to sit.** Make sure your partner can lean back and cuddle up—close enough to talk, but far enough so he can make the move closer to you at his own discretion. The ideal: one of those **L**-shaped couches, where you can sit almost directly facing someone, but you have a back to lean on and no barriers to keep you apart if you choose to move in closer.

3. **Have a handy place to put a glass.** Sitting around holding a drink, figuring out where to put it so it won't leave a stain, is agony.

4. **Keep your apartment on the warm side.** Women are more comfortable if it's warmer. And if your guest is a male, this will encourage him to remove his jacket and tie.

5. **Have several lights in the room.** Having only one source of light can blind the person sitting in the wrong direction.

6. **Keep your place small, personalized, and homey.** Sterile, modernistic environments are for showing how financially

prosperous you are, not for flirting. Successful flirts say that having silly books, games, or knickknacks also helps break the ice.

**7. Don't forget the kitchen.** Successful flirts agree that love often blossoms first in the kitchen, even in a three-foot kitchen. While making the coffee or opening the ice cream, you can say lots of things that might seem forward in another place. So a kitchen table and two chairs might be the most important furniture you can acquire.

**8. Throw out those pillows.** You know those throw pillows your mother said would perk up that ancient living room sofa? Get rid of them. Guests are afraid to lean back on them, and they only make for a more stilted atmosphere.

**9. A bar set up in the living room? No.** Although this is a nice gesture, it looks too professional and preplanned. Grabbing the brandy from the cupboard puts your flirting partner more at ease than having a sterling silver bucket of ice and glasses out and ready.

**10. Mementos of previous relationships should all be removed from view or even from superficially hidden niches.**

Maybe your partner will decide to do a bit of sleuthing while you check your answering machine to see if any previous flirting partners have called you back.

**11. Clear out your medicine cabinet.** You want the thrill of breaking the news about your various maladies to a *committed* partner, not having a strange flirting partner scooping you with a half-true story.

## IN THE OFFICE

You'll want to appear professional, but not coldhearted. Which means that in amongst all the highly decorated pieces, there should be a few plants, a nicely framed picture of an older person (why put in your current love unless you are absolutely certain?), and, if you have children, a framed, original Crayola drawing. This wins over just about everyone.

The office should have a special sitting corner as well, even if you have to drag the chairs from in front of your desk over to it. Have a place that is more personal, if you want to flirt.

One outrageous flirt, a secretary, has on her desk a bowl of Lifesavers that she refills every week. She said everyone from the president to the elevator operators would mosey over and take one. Yes, this was a little expensive, but it put her desk at the hub of activity. She raised her flirting visibility enormously.

In decorating, less is often more. But in flirtatious environments, *more* is more. A pleasant clutter and variety of personality pieces, which give evidence of your interests, can provoke comment and make you utterly appealing.

# ♡ VI ♡
# THE SUCCESSFUL FLIRT

# 34

# 12 Qualities of a Successful Male Flirt

A SUCCESSFUL MALE FLIRT MUST FIRST AND FOREMOST EXUDE A PATIENT AND UNDEMANDING STANCE ABOUT FLIRTING AND COURTSHIP. The more he wants to flirt, the more he must rein in his energies. The *Playboy* Man, the Marlboro Man, and even the Right-Stuffed Astronauts are, actually, the antithesis of successful flirts. They are overequipped. Women don't want to contend with someone wrapped up in an image, especially one out of the late fifties and early sixties. As every woman senses, a man who is flirting conspicuously is actually doing this to impress other men.

Obvious aggression and blatant remarks about a woman's sexuality are not flattering or appealing to women. Any man who tries this will fail, especially if there are other men vying for a woman's attention, because the *next* man who comes on the scene and who is the least bit less aggressive, will sweep the woman off her feet.

Men who get the most from flirting tend not to advertise their triumphs. Maybe they don't want to admit they *are* flirting, which is also part of the magic flirting formula. Here, then, are twelve qualities that describe the successful male flirt.

1. He is comfortable in his environment and projects ease and stability.

2. He has a soft voice.

3. He is confident enough to reveal something about himself.

4. He has a real interest in talking with a woman about rather mundane things.

5. He is honest and can be counted on to do what he says he'll do.

6. He has good manners.

7. He is curious about a woman and wants to know her opinions.

8. He has the ability to tune the world out when the two of you are together.

9. He knows when to end the flirtation.

10. He is affectionate and supportive.

11. He is protective—like a big brother.

12. He knows that the little things count—flowers, a goodnight call, a special restaurant, a magnificent view.

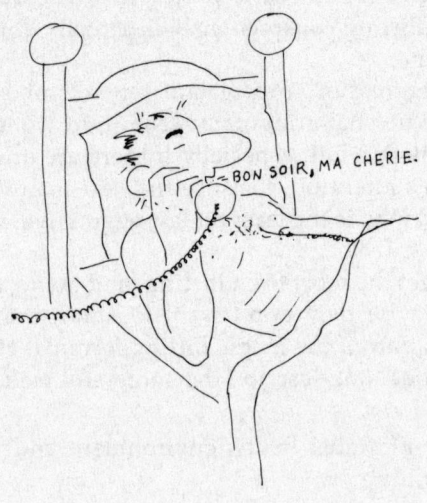

# 35

# 12 Qualities of a Successful Female Flirt

ALTHOUGH PATIENCE AND LOW-KEY FLIRTING TECHNIQUES ARE THE CRITERIA OF THE SUCCESSFUL MALE FLIRT, EXACTLY THE OPPOSITE APPLIES TO WOMEN. Successful female flirts must do two things differently from male flirts. First, when a successful woman flirt decides to zero in on a man, she must repeat her flirtatious gesture at least four or five times. Several fast flirtatious actions work very well with men. Unlike a woman, a man likes to be sure that a female flirt is after *him*, not his buddy. Multiple-shot flirtation seems to answer that concern.

Successful female flirts should also make bold, yet quick, gestures. Whereas men must be subtle or they are perceived as too aggressive, women must be suddenly very bold, then back off completely. The bold action must occur for no more than two or three seconds. In other words, a woman's signals must be far more blatant, be given with greater frequency, but must be much shorter in duration. However, if a woman holds her flirtatious posture more than three seconds, she is committing flirting suicide. There are some successful women flirts who can get a flirtatious intention across in one second. It's important that a woman doesn't muddy her intentions, however. Since they are short, they cannot be indirect. Overdo actions, overdo frequency, but *don't* overdo the time spent flirting. Then, too, there must be a generous space of time (at least three to five minutes) between each flirtatious action. Otherwise a woman appears too bold.

Here are twelve qualities that describe the successful female flirt.

1.  She is successful but doesn't compete with a man.

2.  She maintains a fresh face and interesting style by making small, occasional changes in her appearance—hairstyle, makeup, clothing, and so forth.

3.  She has a self-confident walk.

4.  She is kind.

5.  She makes slow, catlike movements.

6.  She is versatile and brief in her conversation.

7.  She primps.

8.  She has a feminine laugh.

9.  She has a neat, clean appearance.

10.  She doesn't behave like a princess.

11.  She is discreet.

12.  She never offends a man's sense of pride or masculinity.

The successful flirt lives by—

---

### THE FLIRTER'S CODE OF ETHICS

1. Never say hello when you can say hello and flirt at the same time.
2. Never take the short route home, because, at home, there are virtually no chances to flirt at all. While out, the choices are limitless.
3. Never let an old romantic heartache keep you from flirting. Good flirts never regret what they've done, only what they haven't done.

---

Good luck and good flirting!

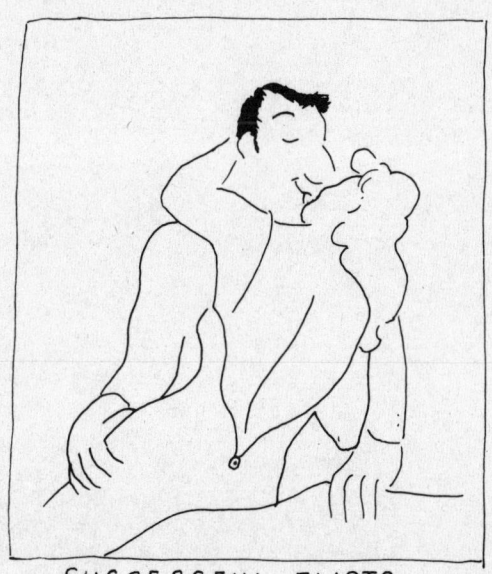

SUCCESSFUL FLIRTS